The Five Laws to Foresee the Future

The Five Laws to Foresee the Future

12 Paradigm Shifts That Will Happen

In the Future of Human Society

Hiroshi Tasaka

Jorge Pinto Books Inc.
New York

This English edition is published in 2009 by Jorge Pinto Books Inc., 151 East 58th Street, New York, N.Y. 10022, U.S.A. under permission of and by arrangement with the author.

This book was originally published in Japanese under the title
"未来を予見する「五つの法則」" by Kobunsha Co., ltd., Tokyo, Japan in 2008.

Cover design: Susan Hildebrand
Translation : Babel Corporation (www.babeltmc.com)

ISBN: 1-934978-15-9
978-1-934978-15-3

This edition of *The Five Laws to Foresee the Future* is published under the Books in Translation series of Jorge Pinto Books Inc.

Dialectic thinking is

the key to foreseeing the future.

Contents

Preface

This book was written for two purposes.
The first is to talk about a method of foreseeing the future in the coming age of uncertainty.
The second is to talk about what kind of future we can foresee by applying this method.

For these purposes, I described in this book the "Five Laws of Dialectic" as the method of foreseeing the future and the future foreseen as "12 paradigm shifts."

However, in fact, this book was written for another hidden purpose.

That is to create a "new style of book" and a "new style of writing" through publishing this book.

Behind that purpose, there are three questions in my mind.

The first question is how will "our styles of writing" change as a result of the Internet revolution spreading worldwide today.
In the age of the Net revolution where many people read and write e-mail, and read and publish ideas through blogs or websites, how will our styles of writing change?

The second question is how will the "English language" change as a result of the Internet revolution.

The English language has become, in fact, the global language by the Net revolution.

But it does not simply mean that American English or British English has become the standard language of the world.

What people all over the world should endeavor to do cooperatively is to create a kind of universal language to be called "global plain English," which is easy to understand for many people around the world who use English as a second language.

The third question is what style of writing will be required to describe "Eastern philosophy" or "Japanese thought" by using "Western language," namely English.

And then, what has emerged from such questions are the following three styles:

1. the style of book that makes use of line feeds and blank lines like a style of e-mail or blogs.
2. the style of writing that uses only plain English, rather than difficult expressions.
3. the style of writing that can describe structurally Eastern philosophy, Japanese thought and the author's original thought.

The unique style of this book, which makes frequent use of line feeds, blank lines, quotation marks and punctuation marks, was created from such efforts.

I hope that readers will enjoy these new styles as well as the contents of this book.

Foreword

The Key to Foreseeing the Future

Lies in "Dialectic Thinking."

The "Five Laws" of Dialectic.

We cannot "predict" the future.
But
we can "foresee" it.

We want to know the future.

Everyone harbors such a thought.

If we could predict the future,
an individual could open up his or her own life.
And businesspersons and executives
could develop their businesses or companies
while politicians and administrators
could bring prosperity to the state and society.

If it were really possible to predict the future,
we could solve many problems facing us.

Everyone harbors such thoughts, such desires.
For that very reason, the world is flooded with
all kinds of books on predicting the future.

But in the coming age,
we must admit to one fact.

We cannot predict the future.

That is an undeniable fact.
And there are three reasons for it.

The first is discontinuity.

Most of the changes that will occur in the coming age
will not be continuous changes.
Discontinuous and dramatic changes,
cut off from the past, will occur.
So the word "evolution" is often used in the world.
In such an age, we cannot predict the future
by extrapolating from the changes of the past.
Just by investigating and analyzing "past tendencies,"
we cannot see the future.
The future will come suddenly cut off from the past.
This is the first reason.

The second is non-linearity.

In addition to discontinuity,
this non-linearity makes prediction even harder.
Even a slight fluctuation in the corner of society
can cause an enormous change of society as a whole.
The metaphor often used for this is
the "butterfly effect."

The three reasons
we cannot predict the future.
Discontinuity, non-linearity, acceleration.

"When a butterfly flutters its wings in Beijing,
a hurricane occurs in New York."
This is the so-called "non-linear effect."
In other words, a slight fluctuation at present
can cause enormous changes in the future.
So if we just look at "current major trends,"
we cannot know the future.
This is the second reason.

The third is acceleration.

This is the age of the "dog year" in which
changes that took 7 years in the past
occur in one year in the present.
And now we have the "mouse year" in which
changes that took 18 years in the past
occur in one year.
Changes of all things have been accelerated.
And in such an age,
when we predict the future,
the future has already gone by.

Therefore,
if we think only of "changes in the near future,"
we actually cannot see the future itself.
This is the third reason.

That is,
"discontinuity,"
"non-linearity,"
"acceleration."

These three factors, in the present time,
make predicting the future extremely difficult.

Then, what should we do?

If we cannot predict the future, what should we do?

Answering this question is the purpose of this book.
So right here in the beginning,
I will present the answer.

We cannot "predict" the future.
But we can "foresee" it.

That is the answer.
Then, what do these words mean?

We cannot predict specific changes.
However,
we can foresee macroscopic trends.

We cannot predict the future.
But we can foresee it.

What do these words mean?

We cannot predict specific changes.
However,
we can foresee macroscopic trends.

That is what they mean.

That is,
"within so many years, this will happen."
"Its scale will be about this much."

We cannot make such a
"quantitative prediction" or
"concrete prediction."

However,
"the world will move in this direction."
"These kinds of trends will appear in society."

We can make such a
"directional foreseeing" or
"macroscopic foreseeing."

That is, we cannot predict detailed changes
that will happen in the future.
But we can foresee major trends
that will occur in the future.

For example, we make a sand pile on the beach,
and pour water on it down from the top.
At that time,
which channels will the water flow down?
No one can predict the channel,
since it depends on chance or fluctuation.
But everyone can foresee one thing clearly.

Water always flows to a lower level.

This is essentially what we call a "macro view."

And, by implementing this macro view,
we can foresee the future.

Then, how can we acquire
this macro view?

**Rather than learning the methods of
predicting the future,
we should learn the laws of world development.**

What we need to do to acquire
this macro view.

It is not simply to expand of our perspective
or to look into the distant future.

There is the most important thing
in order to acquire such a macro view.
What is it?

It is to learn the laws of world development.

By "world" here we mean
all things and beings including
nature, society, human beings.

We should learn the laws that explain
how this world changes, develops, and evolves.

In other words, it is the law that states
"all things in the world
will necessarily develop in this direction."

By learning this,
we can foresee the future
through activating this macro view.

Until now, various methods have been proposed
and used to predict the future.
But rather than learning such "methods"
of predicting the future,
something more important and effective exists:

It is to learn the "laws" about
how the world changes, develops, and evolves.

Then, how can we learn
these laws of world development?

By studying "philosophy."

Philosophy can discern
the basic nature of the world.
And it can gain an insight into the laws
that lie at the basis of
world change, development, and evolution.

By studying philosophy,
we can foresee the future.

If so, what kind of "philosophy" is this?

"Ancient philosophy" already teaches us the "laws" of world development.

It is "dialectic."

That philosophy teaches us
the "laws" of world change, development,
and evolution.

When hearing the word "dialectic,"
most of people will think of a particular philosopher.

The philosopher of German Idealism, Georg Hegel.

His philosophy is called "Hegel's Dialectic."
Among the philosophies created by humankind,
it represents the pinnacle of philosophy
and is the most difficult to understand.
But "dialectic" does not belong only
to Hegel.

In Western philosophy,
its beginning is in
the "Dialogue" of Socrates.

And in modern philosophy,
the German philosopher
Karl Marx's Dialectical Materialism and
the French philosopher Jean-Paul Sartre's
Existentialism also includes the philosophy of dialectic.

However, dialectic is not just discussed in
Western philosophies.
This "dialectic" is discussed
even in Eastern philosophies
having a history of several thousand years.

For example, in the foundations of
Buddhist thought, there is dialectic philosophy.
The Heart Sutra epitomizes this with the words:
"Form itself is emptiness.
Emptiness itself is form."

Taoism, which originated in China,
also discusses dialectic.
It is symbolized by the words:
"Yin ultimately is Yang. Yang ultimately is Yin."

Another example is Zen Buddhism,
which in Japan
attained the most sophisticated depth.
Actually most of the koans, or Zen riddles, teach
the "ultimate confrontation with contradiction."
Thus we can find many instances of dialectic thinking
in the words of Zen.

The "philosophy of dialectic"
teaches us
the "Five Laws" of the development of the world.

In this way, the "ancient philosophies"
created by humankind
have already taught us the laws.

How this world changes, develops, and evolves.
"Dialectic" teaches us these laws as
wisdom of humankind from the past.

Then, what kind of philosophy is "dialectic?"

The purpose of this book is to relate this
in a simple style.

At first, I shall introduce the laws of dialectic
as the "Five Laws."

These laws
are the laws of world development
that have been stated in various thoughts
and philosophies
ancient and modern, of the East and the West.

The "Five Laws" of Dialectic.

The First Law
The law of development through "spiral process."

The world develops as if it were climbing a spiral staircase.

The Second Law
The law of development through "negation of negation."

Current "trends" always "reverse" themselves in the future.

The Third Law
The law of development through
"transformation from quantity to quality."

When the "quantity" exceeds a specific level,
the "quality" changes dramatically.

The Fourth Law
The law of development through
"interpenetration of opposing objects."

Things which oppose and compete with each other
come to resemble each other.

The Fifth Law
The law of development through
"sublation of contradiction."

Contradiction is the driving force
for the development of the world.

Then, let us discuss these "Five Laws."

Chapter One

The World Develops as if
It were Climbing a Spiral Staircase.

The First Law

The Law of Development through
"Spiral Process."

> **The world develops as if
> it were climbing
> a spiral staircase.**

Then, what is the "First Law" of dialectic?

It is
**the law of development through
"spiral process."**

This is, in a word, the following law:

**The world develops as if
it were climbing a spiral staircase.**

That is, the progress and development of
everything in the world
does not proceed ever upward in a straight line.
It all develops in a spiral, in a circular movement,
as if climbing a spiral staircase.

That is what this law teaches us.
What then happens in this "spiral development?"

We can understand this if we watch people
climbing a spiral staircase.

If we look at them from the side,
the people are going up the spiral stairs.
That is, as they proceed to a higher position,
they seem to be "progressing and developing."

However, if we look at them from high above,
as the people are climbing up the spiral stairs,
they are going around the stairs once and
returning to their original place.
That is, it looks as if
they seem to be "reviving and restoring"
to their old position.

But if we look carefully,
they have not simply returned to their original position.
By climbing up the spiral stairs, the people
will certainly have reached one level higher than before.

That is the law of development through
"spiral process."

Now, if this spiral development
is the basic nature and
basic form of all things in the world,
just what will happen as a result?

"Progress and development" and "revival and restoration" occur simultaneously.

"Progress and development" and
"revival and restoration"
occur simultaneously.

That is what this law teaches us.

In other words, that means the following:

The "evolution to the future" and
"regression to the origin" of the world
occur simultaneously.

Such words as "progress" and "evolution" are
often used in the world.

But when we use these words,
we unconsciously harbor a misunderstanding.

Progress and evolution
are linear developments towards the future.

Consequently, progress and evolution
are processes in which old things are discarded.

People always harbor this misunderstanding.

However, neither progress nor evolution
are simply processes in which new things are born.
Nor are they simply processes that throw out old things.

They are processes by which old things are
revived with new value added.

Processes by which old things are
revived with new forms.

And actually this present age
is replete with examples of this spiral development.

This spiral development,
if we look at the world around us,
can be seen anywhere we look.

Why is it so?

The Internet revolution
has revived
the "nostalgic business models."

The Internet revolution.

Because it happened.
The "Net revolution" that began in the mid-1990s.
It gave birth to many examples of
this spiral development.

For example,
"e-commerce" which uses the Net to trade in goods.
Then, what are the advanced business models
that were born from this e-commerce?

The Net auction.
The reverse auction.

These are the business models.

An "auction" refers to a "bidding" method.
It is a method that
when selling a product,
the seller gathers many buyers to bid on it
and sells to the highest bidder
instead of selling at a fixed price.

A "reverse auction" refers to a "limit price" method.
It is a method that
when buying a product,
the buyer indicates the price he or she is willing to pay
and buys it if a seller appears who accepts that price
instead of buying at a fixed price.

Currently in e-commerce,
the number of people trading products has increased
who use these advanced services
called auctions and reverse auctions.

But if we think of it, we notice something strange.

This is by no means a "new business model."

Because if we think about it,
these methods of "bidding" and "limit price"
have been around for a long time.
In the old days,
in the corners of village and town marketplaces,
this trading by bidding and limit price
was always going on.

That is, these methods of auctions and reverse auctions
are by no means new business models.

Rather, they are nostalgic business models.

If so, why did these nostalgic models
fade from view?

The Internet revolution
is triggering
the "spiral development" of the market.

Because of "rationalization."

Because, as capitalism developed,
markets became "rationalized."

Trading goods by such methods as
"bidding" and "limit price."
It was a business custom and was going on daily
in the old days, in village and town marketplaces.

However, as capitalism developed and markets expanded,
markets were no longer just
"marketplaces in the corners of towns"
and they became "regional marketplaces."
Then, they became "nationwide marketplaces."
And, along with this development,
bidding and limit price
became "inefficient" as well as "non-rational."

For this reason,
such "inefficient business models" disappeared.

No.
Let us be more precise.

For a time
such inefficient business models disappeared.

But, capitalism developed further,
markets reached a global scale, and
"nationwide marketplaces" became
"worldwide marketplaces."
And as capitalism developed,
the information revolution advanced.
So, informatization of the market advanced,
and rationalization of the market
developed to its limits.

However, just at that stage,
a revolution occurred that pushed
capitalist development even further.

It was the Net revolution.

And, through the arrival of this revolution,
oddly enough, the nostalgic business models of
bidding and limit price revived in the markets.
In the form of the Net auctions and reverse auctions,
these business models that had once disappeared
came back to life.

Now, what happened?

Spiral development of the market.

The capitalist market made one turn around
the spiral staircase.
For this reason, business models that had once
disappeared revived.
The nostalgic business models have come back to life.

But here we must realize
an important matter.

"Spiral development"
is not simply
"revival and restoration."

Spiral development is not simply
"revival and restoration."

We must realize this.

As stated earlier, spiral development
is a development as if climbing a spiral staircase.

That is, looking from above,
it seems that we are returning to the same place,
but from the side,
we have actually climbed up one level.
That means something is definitely
progressing and developing.

For example,
the auctions and reverse auctions
that were revived in e-commerce.
The old methods of bidding and limit price
have not revived in exactly their original forms.

For sure, they have climbed up one level.
Certainly they have progressed and developed.

Because the bidding and limit price in the old markets
could only function at most with
several hundred people.

But the auctions and reverse auctions
that were revived in e-commerce
are markets on the Internet.

For that reason, it is possible to sell and buy goods
targeting the millions and billions of people on earth.
And as a result of the global distribution revolution,
even people on the other sides of the globe
can trade instantly with
a minimum of time, effort and cost.

This means that
"we have climbed up one spiral step."

That is, in this spiral development,
we have actually climbed up one level
and something is definitely
progressing and developing.

If we overlook this,
we misunderstand the meaning of spiral development.
We would take it as
simple "revival of something old" or
"restoration to the past."

"We climb up one spiral step."

Actually, this is a vital perspective
when foreseeing the future
through the application of the law of spiral development.

**When there is revival and restoration,
something necessarily
progresses and develops.**

Let us look at one more example of spiral development.

This is the "Net-based group purchase."

Now, in e-commerce, this business model of
the Net-based group purchase is expanding.
It is the business model that when selling goods,
the seller will attract customers by saying
"there would be a 20% discount,
if a hundred people can gather to make the purchase."

Now, the Net shops that are expanding their sales by using
this system of the Net-based group purchases
have increased.
However, this is also a nostalgic business model.
If we think about it carefully,
this type of "group purchase"
has been around for a long time.

It is the "consumer cooperative" (or "co-op").

Local people or workers get together to order products
needed for their living.
By doing this, they bring down the product price.
Such a system has existed from long ago.

But, as the distribution revolution has advanced
and price competition has progressed through
volume purchasing by major supermarkets,
such a system of group purchase by the co-op
has become out of the mainstream in the world.

However, with the emergence of e-commerce,
the group purchase system has revived
as a Net-based business model.
That is, it has come back to life.

And, this naturally was not a simple revival of
something old.

That is because, in the Net-based group purchase system,
which differs from the co-op system,
the people participating in group purchase
do not have to belong to special organizations,
or to gather in special localities or workplaces,
and anyone can freely participate by responding to
invitations over the Internet.

In this way,
the emergence of the business model of
the Net-based group purchase is also not simply
"revival of something old" or "restoration to the past."
Rather, it has climbed up one step on the spiral staircase.
Something has progressed and developed.

Then, are these examples of spiral development
occurring only in the market?

Not so.

E-learning
has revived
a "nostalgic educational system."

This spiral development
has not only been occurring in the market.
It has been occurring in various forms
in the domains of both society and culture.

If so, in society, what kind of
spiral development has been occurring?

For example, in the field of education,
the Net revolution has spread "e-learning,"
which uses the Internet.
As a result, it has become possible
to receive various kinds of education
at home, at a time of one's choosing.

However, the essence of e-learning
is not simply a system of distance learning.
Then what is it?

It is a system of "individualized learning."

That is, in other words, e-learning
is an educational system where individual learners
can acquire knowledge according to their own
interests and abilities, individually, at their own paces.

In contrast, in conventional education,
despite learners each having different
interests and abilities,
they were required to follow the same teacher,
the same curriculum, and the same textbook,
and to study at the same pace.

This was a common system called "group education,"
which was conducted
not only in elementary and middle schools
but also in the academies, professional schools
and private seminars.

However, the newly emerged form of e-learning
is a system in which learners can individually and freely
choose fields of their own interests,
and can study at their own pace
matching their individual abilities.
That is, learners can search for websites
offering education in subjects of personal interest,
and can select educational institutions
offering the curricula most suitable for them.
It is an individualized learning system
where learners are free to choose their learning style
whether to study at a fixed time every day or
to concentrate on their study on a weekend.

And then, if we think about it carefully,
this individualized learning system
is a revival of a nostalgic educational system.

Why is that?

**The regression of an educational system has occurred,
from "mass, uniform, and heteronomous"
to "individual, free, and autonomous."**

That is because
all of the educational systems in societies in the past
were individualized learning systems.

The educational systems in past societies
differed from the present ones.
They were not the systems in which
a mass of pupils and students of the same age
gathered, and received education uniformly
following a heteronomous curriculum.

For example, in medieval European society
children of the aristocracy
received education through the "private tutor system."

This was a system in which
a single teacher was in charge of a single pupil
individually, and offered education freely
following an autonomous curriculum
by taking into account
the interests and abilities of the pupil.

Also, during the feudal age in Japan,
the common people would receive their education
at "temple schools" ("*Terakoya*").

In this temple school system,
people of various ages and social classes
would gather at places such as temples spontaneously,
and study individually and autonomously
based on their interests and abilities.

That is, if we look back at the history of humankind,
the modern educational system by no means has
a long history.

Educational systems that emphasize
"the masses," "uniformity," and "heteronomy."

Such systems by no means have a long history.

Educational systems that emphasize
"the individual," "freedom," and "autonomy."

Such systems were, from a historical viewpoint,
the mainstream for a long time.

But, in the transition to modern "industrialized society,"
as the need increased to provide education
efficiently to large numbers of people,
the educational systems that emphasized
the mass, uniform and heteronomy
became the mainstream.

Consequently, the educational systems that emphasized
the individual, freedom and autonomy found in
the private tutor and the temple schools disappeared.

Old educational systems
are coming back
with "new value."

However,
these old educational systems of the private tutors
and the temple schools are now coming back
along with the progress and development of society.
They are coming back in the form of e-learning
through the Net revolution.

Because, by making use of the Internet,
e-learning realized the educational system in which
everyone can receive one-to-one education at low cost.

Especially, at the beginning,
e-learning was run with e-mail,
but recently, the popularization of broadband
made videoconferencing possible,
then, it has enabled to not only impart "knowledge,"
but also impart "tacit knowing" inexpressible in words.

That is, education through a private tutor system,
which could not be offered in the past except to
the aristocracy and wealthy families,
is now easily obtainable at low cost by everyone
through e-learning.

Also, by utilizing the Internet,
e-learning enables anyone to take advantage of
an educational system where people can study
at their own pace, in accordance with subjects of
their own interests and abilities.

That is, the education offered in the past through
temple schools and tutors can now be obtained easily
by anyone without having to live in a particular location.

However, this also is a spiral development.
It is not just a revival.

The e-learning system is not limited
to the knowledge held by a single private tutor
or only to the books in a single temple school,
but affords instruction in which people can freely
acquire knowledge from all over the world,
and learn from the best teachers in the world.

In reality, major universities in the world
such as MIT and Stanford
now provide over the Internet
free movies of their lectures
and anyone can access those lectures.

This is precisely
the revival of an old educational system
at a sophisticated level.
It is none other than the spiral development of
the educational system.

E-mail
has revived
the culture of the "letter."

Let us take one more example of spiral development
in society.

It is "e-mail."

Convenient e-mail,
now used freely by most people in advanced countries.
But if we think about it carefully,
this is a revival of the old "letter."

In human history in the past,
the letter was the major means of communication.
And everyone wrote letters to
communicate with people far away.

However, because of the appearance of the "telephone,"
that culture of communication changed.
This is because most people became able to easily use
the telephone as a means of communication.

For this reason, the habit of writing letters
no longer became the mainstream in the world.

Compared to the telephone, the letter is a medium
that requires time and effort to write and send.
So this old means of communication came to be
avoided by most people.

But, with the emergence of e-mail,
that culture of the letter revived.

To write messages by "text"
and deliver them to other people.

That "nostalgic culture of communication"
revived and again became the mainstream.

However, this is not a simple revival.
This also is a spiral development.

Because e-mail differs from the letters of the past
in some of the following ways:
E-mail can easily be written with
a personal computer or cell phone.
E-mail can reach people anywhere on earth instantly.
E-mail can send simultaneously the same message to
many people.
Furthermore, voice and movies can be sent
by voice mail and movie mail.

Because the culture of the letter has revived
accompanied by new values as mentioned above.

The Internet revolution
has revived
the culture of the "volunteer."

In this way, what the Internet brought us
was a revival of a nostalgic thing
that existed in markets and societies in the past.
It was none other than
a spiral development of the world.

And, actually, the Internet itself
came, embracing a "nostalgic culture."

What is that?

The culture of the volunteer.

The new medium of the Internet,
from its very beginning,
has embraced the culture of the volunteer.
It is a culture in which
people spontaneously help and assist each other
not because of being forced upon it by others
nor being motivated by monetary compensation.

For example, the "knowledge communities"
that emerged in great number owing to the Net revolution.

These are the Net communities where
a large number of people
sharing interests in similar topics
gather on the Internet.

In such communities, if someone posts a question,
other participating members in that community
offer various opinions and special knowledge
addressed to that question.
In other words, they offer their valuable knowledge.

But, that is not because they have obligation or
responsibility to answer those questions,
nor they expect some kind of monetary compensation for
answering them.
The reason is simply that members feel like assisting
other members who post their questions,
and feel like answering them spontaneously.
This is because such a volunteer culture,
namely a mutual assistance culture,
resides in this community.

However, this volunteer culture
residing in the Net community
is also a "nostalgic culture."

It is a culture that
always existed in the local communities in the past.
In every area of the world,
there was a culture in which the people in the region
helped and assisted each other.
And it was also a culture of a "whole society."

Then, why did this culture fade from view?

**From now,
a revival of the culture of the "volunteer"
will occur on a worldwide scale.**

This is because of the development of capitalism.

The development caused
a massive shift of the working population,
depopulation of rural areas,
and population concentration in large cities.

In the midst of such changes,
the culture of the volunteer,
which had its roots deeply in local communities,
was lost.
The volunteer culture, found in all corners of society,
began to disappear.

However, the Net revolution
has revived the once-lost volunteer culture.
It has revived the culture of the volunteer again
all over society through the Net community.

This is, in a sense,
a spiral development of culture.

In the past society, the culture of the volunteer
spread its roots deeply through the corners of society
along with the activity of
mutual assistance by the people.
However, along with the development of capitalism,
all kinds of services now were becoming commodities.

A culture in which all kinds of services were
convertible to "currency" spread widely.
And with this, the volunteer culture declined.

But, with the arrival of the Net revolution,
that culture came back to life.
This was precisely
a spiral development at the level of culture.
The nostalgic culture of the past has revived.

However, again,
this is not a simple revival but a spiral development.

Because, in this knowledge community, people are able to
cooperate with people on the other side of the Earth.
In the old community, mutual assistance was limited to
a few hundred people because of geographical restrictions.
But, in this new community,
millions of people across the globe
can help and assist each other.

The symbolic example of this is the "Linux community."
It is the knowledge community in which engineers
around the world gather and continually improve on
the operating system called "Linux,"
which everyone can freely use.
Responding to the invitation of a single engineer,
Linus Torvalds, thousands of engineers are gathering
voluntarily from around the world and
are offering their knowledge and wisdom
day and night without compensation.

This is an actual revival of
the volunteer culture on a worldwide scale.

Not only "nostalgic things" have revived, but "nostalgic things that became convenient" have revived.

In this way, in the market and in society,
as well as in the cultural domain,
"nostalgic things" have revived.
And a restoration of "nostalgic things" is taking place:

The business models of the bidding and limit price.
The educational systems of the private tutor, and
the temple school.
The cultures of the letter and the volunteer.

These are the nostalgic things that have been revived.

However, when we look at their spiral development,
there is one thing that we must not forget.

The various nostalgic things that are now being revived.

They are not merely nostalgic things.

They are "nostalgic things that became convenient."

This must not be forgotten.

"Nostalgic things that became convenient."

Actually, this viewpoint is extremely important.

Because, in markets and societies,
when "spiral development" occurs
and "revival" of old things happens,
most of them revive as
"nostalgic things that became convenient."

We should remember again
the law of development through "spiral process."

In spiral development,
we do not merely return to the original point
by going around the spiral staircase.
When we return to the origin,
always we have ascended to a position
one step higher.
Always, something has progressed and developed.

In many cases,
things have become more rational, more efficient
and easier to use, and have added new functions.
Consequently they have become more convenient.

That is, a nostalgic thing has returned to become
something convenient.

This is what happens in spiral development.

Again, this must not be forgotten.

Due to the global environmental problems a nostalgic culture of "resource recycling" has revived.

Now, will such spiral development
occur only in the world of the Net revolution?

Is it also true that the spiral development
occurred only in such familiar situations as
products and services in the markets?

Not so.
This spiral development has occurred
outside of the world of the Net revolution
in many ways.
This has been occurring on a grand scale
in social systems, political institutions,
and economic principles.

"Resource recycling," for example.

The importance of resource recycling
has received strong emphasis,
along with the deepening of the
crisis in the global warming.
However,
when we look back in history,
this resource recycling
also is a revival of an old culture.

In the past,
in ages when economy was relatively undeveloped,
"resources" were extremely valuable for people.
For that reason, in society
it was a common sense practice to recycle resources.
In their daily lives,
people treated resources as precious
and reused them without throwing them away.

But, as economy developed,
and resources became available at low cost,
culture underwent a change.
The so-called
mass-production mass-consumption culture
became the mainstream.
It was the age of the value system that
"mass consumption of resources indicates wealth."

However, the obstacles this kind of society encountered
are the environmental problems such as global warming.

The consumption of resources on a massive scale
results in the massive discharge of
carbon dioxide into the atmosphere.
As this came to be widely understood,
the culture of resource recycling has revived.

In that sense, this resource recycling also
was a regression to the origin of
this old and nostalgic "social system."

However, after all,
the essence of the regression is spiral development,
so, at the same time,
an evolution to the future are occurring.

"Resource recycling" at the present time is becoming a resource recycling that has achieved spiral development.

For example, when we look at resource recycling
at the individual level,
an evolution to the future is obvious.

In the old days,
if someone recycled needless products and
tried to find people to use them,
finding a person who needs the product
would be very difficult
because it requires time, effort and cost to do so.

For that purpose, the only thing that could be done
was to call on one of the few specialists in recycling
or open his or her own free market.
There were no other good methods.

However, at the present time,
in order to carry out such recycling,
an excellent method has emerged.

The "Net auction."

By utilizing an Internet auction service,
it is possible to easily discover
someone who needs these items
without spending time, effort, and cost.

Also, inexpensive rapid services have been developed
such as home delivery
for delivering the product to the other person.

In this way, in resource recycling as well,
regression to the origin and evolution to the future
are taking place simultaneously.
Nostalgic things are reviving,
which has become convenient.

This is not only at the individual level.
It can also be seen even in social systems as a whole.

For example, now, in comparison to the past,
there exists a high level of technologies, systems,
institutions and cultures, for resource recycling.

In addition to the Net auction sales system
mentioned above,
resource recycling has come back with
new values added, as follows:

Technology for recycling paper and plastics.
Development of easy to recycle eco-materials.
Separate recovery systems for reuse.
Introduction of systems of incentive for reuse.
Heightening of people's consciousness of the environment
and the formation of an environmental culture.

In other words, it is a "revival" accompanied by
new technologies, systems, institutions and cultures.
The old resource recycling system has come back
as a new one, which has achieved spiral development.

Through the Internet revolution
the old and nostalgic "voluntary economy"
has revived.

Such spiral development
has further occurred in economy as well.

It is a revival of the voluntary economy.

Then, what is this voluntary economy?

Actually,
it is the oldest economic principle of humankind.

In capitalist societies of the present day,
the mainstream is the monetary economy
that is based on currency.
For that reason, we unconsciously assume that
the monetary economy is the only economic activity.
However, before currency was invented,
humankind was engaged in economic activity.

If so, what kind of economic principles existed
prior to the monetary economy based on currency?

It was the barter economy
based on the exchange of goods.

Then, what kind of economic principles
existed before this?

It was the voluntary economy.

It means the "gift economy," in which
people spontaneously give others items of value
through affection or goodwill.
There was an age in which it dominated
human communities and societies.

But, as time passed, the mainstream of economic principles
shifted to the barter economy.
And, through the invention of currency,
it changed into the monetary economy.

However, this does not mean that
the voluntary economy disappeared entirely.

The voluntary economy has always played
a vital role in human history.

For example, activities such as housework,
child care, education in the home,
caring for the elderly, community services,
and others were highly important economic activities
although they did not involve an exchange of money.

For example,
society could not function without education in the home,
with only primary and intermediate education.
Without uncompensated care for the elderly
by their family,
public welfare and medical care
would be limited and insufficient.

Two reasons
for the revival of the
voluntary economy.

In this sense, the voluntary economy
has been a vital economic principle supporting society.

But, for two reasons,
this economy has been
in the position of a shadow economy.

First, because this economic activity
was limited strictly to the narrow domains of
the family and the locality.

Secondly, because it actually was invisible,
since it could not be evaluated
by the objective measure of currency.

However, this situation changed
when the Net revolution happened.

First, in the Net revolution,
the voluntary economy was liberated
from such a narrow domain.

And now, in the domain of the Net community,
people can gather from around the world.

And in this community,
people can share their own wisdom
and collaborate with each other.
Further, such activities can influence
the entire world through the Internet.

Secondly, the Net revolution
has made the voluntary economy visible.

This cannot be indicated
using quantitative measures of currency,
but it has become visible to many people
by means of the Internet.

Then, what will happen as a result of this from now?

The voluntary economy
will expand its influence in the visible form.

In a sense, it is the revival of
the ancient economic principle of community
among humankind.

The old principle of a gift economy,
as it was called in ancient times,
has revived through the Net revolution.
But it has revived through
a "spiral development carrying new value."

And this voluntary economy that has revived,
in fact, will evolve into a new economic principle
by merging with the monetary economy.

This will be discussed in detail in Chapter 6.

**The spiral development of things
is a subject not only for the historian but also for
the manager, the administrator, and the politician.**

However, the reader who has read up to this point
most likely harbors one doubt in his or her mind.

> Why should we discuss dialectic now?
> Why should we talk about
> the law of spiral development now?
>
> If it is a basic law of development of the world,
> the spiral development of things
> would have been occurring since old times.
> The revival of nostalgic things
> would have been occurring.
> And many people should have already
> noticed this.
> Nevertheless,
> why should we discuss
> the law of spiral development now?

That is exactly correct.
When we look back on world history,
all things have undergone spiral development
from ancient times.

Therefore, outstanding historians,
philosophers and religious leaders throughout the world
have had an insight into this and spoken about it.

However, actually ordinary people
could not see the spiral development.

Because spiral development up until now
had occurred on a "historical scale"
over a long period of time.

Consequently, until now,
this law was an important subject
only for historians, philosophers and religious leaders
who observed changes in the world
on a historical scale.

For ordinary people
who could observe the world
only at the level of their daily life and work,
it was a law of world development
that they could not notice.

But from this point on, this will change.

It will become an important subject
for managers, administrators, and politicians.

Indeed, it will become an important subject also
for businesspersons and ordinary people.

Why is this?

Because "symbolic words" are now coming into use.

In the age of the "dog year," society is beginning to run up the spiral staircase.

The "dog year."
The "mouse year."

That is, changes that used to take 7 years
in the past, now take one year.
Furthermore, changes that used to take 18 years
in the past, now take one year.

The speed of changes in the world
now has accelerated greatly,
as expressed by such words.

As a result, then, what has happened
with these changes?

They have become "visible."

The spiral developments in the world
have now become visible.

Until now, spiral developments that occurred
in the world were invisible to most people.

Because a human life was short.

For certain, spiral developments have been occurring
since old times.
But these were on the order of several centuries,
taking place very slowly.
So we, as individuals,
could not see these spiral developments.

In other words,
compared to the lengths of our lives as humans,
the speed of spiral developments were very slow.
For this reason, we could not see them.

However, history has now entered
the age of the "dog year."
And changes in the world
have accelerated considerably.
So, even in our daily life and work,
we now can witness spiral developments in the world.

To use a metaphor,
we are now "running up" the spiral staircase.

Up until now,
we certainly were climbing up a spiral staircase.
But, since we were climbing up that staircase
much too slowly, over our short lifespan, we were able to
climb up only a few steps of the staircase.
We passed away without even noticing
that it was a spiral staircase.

However, now we are meeting the age
in which we run up that spiral staircase.

For that reason, we can witness various kinds of
spiral developments in our daily life and work.

The age has arrived
when vision, policy, and strategy
immediately become obsolescent.

Therefore, from now we are entering a new age.

It is the age in which we can observe
the spiral development of the world
in a single human life.
Moreover, it is the age in which we witness
the spiral development of the world
in our daily lives.

We are entering such an age.

However, this fact, on the other hand,
forces politicians, administrators and managers
to confront a vexing problem.

It is the problem of
"obsolescence of vision, policy, and strategy."

For example, policies that the government established
by predicting the changes in society and
strategies that companies formulated
by predicting changes in the market
immediately become obsolescent.

They are faced with this problem.

The reason for this obviously is the "dog year."
It is in the fact that the speed of changes
in the world has accelerated.

In the age when changes in the world proceeded slowly,
these changes did not pose great errors,
even if they were considered as "linear changes."

On a macro scale, even if it was a spiral development,
on a micro scale, it would appear as a linear development.

That is because
even if we climbed up the spiral staircase,
if we look only at its handrails,
it appears as if the changes were linear.

For this reason,
in government policy and in corporate strategy as well,
we assumed that the tendencies of change
in current society and the market would continue
as before, and even if we assume the current changes
into the future as linear extensions, no great errors were
generated from such predictions.

However, it is different now,
in the age of the "dog year."

Compared with the past,
since spiral development occurs over a short time span,
such predictions would not hit their marks.

According to the spiral staircase metaphor,
we intended to climb to "the east,"
but before we know it
we are climbing to "the west."

Things that have disappeared
have not disappeared because
they lost their "reason for existence."

Consequently, in the age where
spiral development has accelerated,
politicians, administrators and executives
formulating their visions, policies and strategies
have to construct their plans by foreseeing
what kind of spiral development will occur in society,
the markets, and the business world,
and what kind of new value will be added,
and when it will occur.

Then, how can we foresee such events?

However, in order to foresee them,
it is necessary to solve two misunderstandings
concerning spiral development.

Now, what is the first misunderstanding?

Why have the "old things" disappeared?

It is a misunderstanding about this notion.

Actually, we have a tendency to think
in the following way when something
has disappeared from circulation.

It disappeared
because it lost its reason for existence.

However, actually this is not true.
Because, in the midst of changes of the times,
when something disappears from circulation,
the only thing that has disappeared
is its "surface phenomenon."
It does not at all mean that it has
lost its "reason for existence."

Hegel instructs us about this with the following words:

"Whatever exists, is rational."

What do these words of Hegel tell us?

"Whatever actually exists in the world
necessarily has meaning."

That is what he tells us.

That is, out of all the things that existed in this world,
there is not a single thing
that existed despite having absolutely no meaning.
It has merely disappeared from the surface of society,
since the magnitude of its meaning has changed
and its relative importance has diminished
as time changes and society changes.

It has not disappeared because it lost its meaning.
It merely faded away because its
"degree of importance" had diminished.

Then, why has its degree of importance declined?

As "rationalization" and "streamlining" advance, "older systems" which had once disappeared come back to life.

This is because of rationalization and streamlining.

When societies, markets and companies,
as well as products and services change in their demand
for rationalization and streamlining,
among the various "functions" that these have,
"functions of high importance" are
assigned preference and are strengthened, while
"functions of low importance" are
abandoned to be realized later, and
occasionally fade from view.

However, as rationalization and streamlining progress,
functions with a high degree of importance
are fully realized,
therefore the emphasis shifts to functions
that had been considered of
lower importance until now.
And a movement arises to bring them into practice.

That is the reason for their revival occurring.

That is, when functions of high importance
are realized and become widespread,
a chance for the revival of once disappeared
"functions of low importance" comes.

This is the reason why
"things that have disappeared" come back to life.

The letter and the telephone are examples of this.
The letter has a number of advantages over the telephone.
"We can write while thinking," "we can keep records,"
"we do not interrupt our addressee's time."
These are the advantages it has.
But, it has several disadvantages
compared with the telephone.
"It takes time to write,"
"it takes time to deliver," "a record is left behind."

Consequently,
when we compare these advantages and disadvantages,
in an age when promptness is highly valued,
the means of communication by letter
lost its major position of importance for a while.
That is why the telephone whose main feature is
"promptness" came to play a major role.

However, conditions changed by the emergence of e-mail.
The means of communication by letter had
acquired "promptness," and for this reason,
it revived to its original major position.

That is, the means of communication by letter
had its own advantages, and reasons for existence.
But, in the change to a period where
promptness and streamlining are needed,
the "priority order" of its "advantage" declined.
And there was a major shift to the telephone
as a means of communication.

However, by the emergence of e-mail,
featuring promptness and streamlining,
the culture of the letter revived again.

The nationwide uniform distribution revolution has regressed to "individualism" and "regionalism."

Now let us discuss the most advanced case of
the "distribution revolution" in Japan.

This is the evolution of the "convenience store."

Convenience stores can be found
all over Japan at the present time.
Their history is also a history of
"rationalization" and "streamlining."

So, what was the situation
prior to the appearance of the convenience store?

There were many individual stores in each region
and a large number of stores existed which
had the culture of the locality and
reflected the personality of the owners.

However,
under the banner of the distribution revolution,
rationalization and streamlining,
the convenience store appeared.
It pursued absolute rationalization and streamlining of
retail services, through introducing information systems
such as "POS" (point of sale) as well as
the offering of a nationwide uniform type of service.

But, in the midst of this distribution revolution,
what disappeared by becoming hobbled through this
rationalization and streamlining was
the "individualism" of the small stores,
which valued the individuality of each shop,
and the "regionalism," in which vendors made their shops
reflect local culture.

However, this does not mean at all
that the reason for existence for such style
as individualism and regionalism has been lost.

In order to promote the distribution revolution,
"individualism" and "regionalism" received a low priority.
And it was demanded as a top priority to engage in
rationalization and streamlining and provide
products and services of nationwide uniform quality.

But, as the distribution revolution progressed,
and convenience stores appeared nationwide,
now that rationalization and streamlining have
adequately progressed in these shops,
there is a revival of the individualism and regionalism.

Because the most advanced convenience stores in Japan
have now begun to engage in creating shops that reflect
the environment of the towns and incorporating
the owners' ideas to add character to the shops.

But the revival of individualism and regionalism does not
mean simply that the traditional local shops will revive.
After all, what will revive is a new kind of
individualism and regionalism, which has achieved
spiral development through implementing
leading edge information systems and operating manuals.

Functions which had once disappeared due to rationalization and streamlining will necessarily revive.

So what has happened?

Here also, functions that had once disappeared
due to rationalization and streamlining
came back to life,
since rationalization and streamlining
had reached a certain stage.

Now, what has happened
from the viewpoint of dialectic?

The spiral development of
"homogenization" and "individualization."

That is what has happened.

In the beginning, the stores, which once had an
"individual" character in each region and shop,
aimed at nationwide homogenization
in the midst of the rationalization and streamlining
stemming from the distribution revolution.

However, since this homogenization
progressed to a certain stage,
it went around the spiral staircase and headed again
in the direction of individualization.

That is, it went through the following
spiral development process.

Homogenization in order to achieve rationalization.
Reversal at the end point of rationalization.
Regression from homogenization to individualization.

And this kind of phenomenon of spiral development of
homogenization and individualization
could be seen not only in the convenience store
but also everywhere in society and the market.

In general, when seeing society and the market
from a macro view, it often happens that things,
which once disappeared in the need for rationalization,
move again in the direction of revival
when rationalization reaches its end point.

So, when something disappears
through a widespread change,
we should not conclude that
"it disappeared because it lost its reason for existence."

Rather, we should deeply consider
the meaning and reason for existence of
what has disappeared.

Because, by doing this, we will be able to see.

What will revive from now on?

The "future" will become visible to us.

**In evolution,
"old things" do not disappear.
They coexist and live with "new things."**

Now, what is the second misunderstanding
with regard to spiral development?

What is evolution?

It is a misunderstanding about this question.

This word "evolution" originally is a term from biology.
And, it does not mean merely "continuous changes,"
but "discontinuous jumps."

Recently, also regarding societies, markets and companies,
due to the fact that they have achieved dramatic changes,
it is common to use this word for such things as
"evolution into a knowledge society,"
"evolution into a customer-centric market" and
"evolution into a virtual company."

However, the use of the word evolution here in this way,
when referring to
society, the market and companies,
and even to products and services,
unfortunately is accompanied by
one misunderstanding.

In evolution,
old things disappear.
And new things replace them.

That is the misunderstanding.

However,
in considering the meaning of the word evolution,
we must also understand one more important matter.

Because in the process of evolution,
actually, one more major thing occurs,
not from the perspective of
the "evolution of individual biological species,"
but from the perspective of
the "evolution of ecosystems as a whole."

In evolution,
old things do not disappear.
They coexist and live with new things.

Because that also occurs.

The process of evolution is the same,
not from the perspective of
the "evolution of individual technologies and products,"
but from the perspective of
the "evolution of markets and societies as a whole."

Then, what does this mean?

**In the evolution of the book,
it is not the case that all "paper books" disappear
and are replaced by "electronic books."**

To explain the meaning of this expression,
let us look at one easy-to-understand case.

The "evolution of the book."

In the course of the information revolution,
a revolution is progressing even in the world of
book publishing.
In particular, digitization of the book is advancing
and the technology of the electronic book is
spreading rapidly.

The "electronic book" is that we can download its contents
over the Internet and read it on a liquid crystal display
easily viewable.

This is attracting much attention as
the future evolution of the book.

Old "print media,"
such as books, magazines and newspapers,
are now moving towards
new "electronic media," which are digitized and
sold on the Internet.
This is a very rational direction to follow,
as well as an inevitable one.

This is because electronic media
have the following merits:

"No cost for production and storage."
"No need of time and effort for sale and purchase."
"Easy to search and select what one wants."

For these reasons, the electronic book
will certainly become popular.
But at the same time,
one important misunderstanding frequently occurs.

> In the future, all paper books will become
> electronic books,
> and all printed media will become
> electronic media.

That is the misunderstanding.

However, this never will happen.

Actually, even 100 years from now,
paper books and publications will remain.

That is because paper books and publications
have their own "rationality"
for their existence.

In the evolution of living things, both "old species" and "new species" coexist together on earth.

For example, it is in the "pleasure" of reading a book.

If we avail ourselves of a book that has classical value,
as we read through it,
enjoying the touch of the paper,
the turning of each page,
we bend our ear deeply to the voice of the author,
converse with one who is so far away,
and engage in a dialogue with our inner self.
Sometimes we are inspired to underline the text,
when it strikes us, to make notes in the margins,
and after we finish reading a book,
we close the cover, and
we are overcome with deep emotion for a while.

This "pleasure of reading a book"
is part of the wonders of a paper book,
and we cannot replace it with anything else.

Of course, even in electronic books,
a function has been developed for turning pages.
Also, methods for underlining and writing notes
have been developed.
But, after all,
it is close but not the same as a paper book.

Consequently, no matter how widely popular
electronic books may become,
the paper book will never disappear.

Both of them necessarily will
differentiate from each other and coexist side-by-side.

This actually is clear when we observe
the shape of evolution in the world of nature.

In Darwin's theory of evolution,
fishes became amphibia,
which in turn evolved into reptiles,
and reptiles into mammals,
and the primates developed from mammals.

And among these primates, apes evolved from monkeys,
and Homo sapiens developed from apes.

However, if we look back on
this grand process of evolution,
even now on the Earth,
fishes, amphibia, reptiles, mammals, monkeys and
human beings all exist.

And all these various forms of life
differentiate from each other and coexist side-by-side
on the Earth.

Of course, sometimes some species may
be naturally selected and disappear.
However, the shape of evolution in the world of nature
is moving in the direction that species increasingly
undergo diversification.

**The essence of evolution
is diversification.
The world increases in diversity.**

This is the essence of evolution.

That is, the essence of evolution is diversification.

In evolution,
it is not true that "old things" simply disappear
and "new things" replace them.

It is a process by which old things from the past and
new things that have just come to life,
by differentiating from each other and
coexisting side-by-side,
has heightened the diversity of the world.

Even if several older forms become
extinct through selection at times,
from a macro view, the world moves towards
diversification based on coexistence.
And as a result, the world becomes
increasingly rich in life.

If so, what happens if we apply this concept to
"evolution of products" in the market?

The evolution of products in the market
does not simply mean that an old product disappears
and a new product takes the majority of market share.
These differentiate from each other and
coexist side-by-side in the same way as living species.
Therefore, both the paper book and the electronic book
will differentiate and coexist.

The paper book will most likely live on
as a medium suitable for
perusing long-favorite classics,
reading favorite poems savoring their word,
and keeping them close at hand.

The electronic book will most likely gain
in popularity as a medium suitable for
the information in dictionaries and encyclopedias
that require search functions,
the recent information that is required
through constant updates,
and the practical data that we need not keep.

In this way, the evolution of products in the market,
seen in a broader perspective, is none other than
"diversification of the product ecosystem."

Both new and old products
differentiate from each other and coexist side-by-side.

That is, in other words,
it means that
the market and society increase in diversity
and become a "rich market" and a "rich society."

**In observing society,
we should consider "what is nostalgic"
and "what became convenient."**

Now, as we have discussed up to now,
in order to foresee the future
by applying the law of spiral development,
there are two things we must
understand correctly.

Why do "old things" fade from view?

What is "evolution?"

When we have understood these two correctly,
we can confront the following two questions:

How can we witness spiral development in the world?
How can we make use of this law of spiral development?

Then, first of all,
how can we witness spiral development in the world?

To begin, we must "observe society."

For example,
it is to see "the most recent trends" and "hit products."
It is to see "new social systems" and "new institutions."

In doing this, we will likely discover
"nostalgic things that became convenient"
among the various things we see.

At such a time, we should think deeply about them.

What is nostalgic?
What has become convenient?

When thinking this,
the "essence" of changes in the world will appear.
The "future" of changes in the world will appear.

Secondly,
how can we make use of
this "law of spiral development?"

Now, in all corners of society or markets,
the spiral development of dialectic is occurring.
If this is so,
how can we apply this law of spiral development?
How can we apply this law
to foresee and create the future?

For this purpose,
when scrutinizing the world around us
and things around us,
we should try thinking based on the "four steps."

We can foresee
the nostalgic things that will revive in the world
by the law of spiral development.

Now, what are the four steps?

First, we should foresee "what will revive?"

This is step one.
As mentioned often up to now,
the law of spiral development
states that evolution to the future and
regression to the origin occur simultaneously
in the processes of change, development and evolution of
society and the market.
So, when we scrutinize these processes,
we can see a revival of nostalgic things.
Consequently, we should first foresee
"what will revive?"

And what should we do for this?

We should see "what has disappeared?"

That is step two.
The fundamental direction of events occurring
in the progress and development of society and the market
is rationalization and streamlining.

Consequently, we should consider "what has disappeared?"
in the flow of this rationalization and streamlining.
We should consider what has disappeared
for not being rational or efficient.

Having considered what has disappeared,
what should we do next?

We should consider "why has it disappeared?"

This is step three.
At this stage of the progress and development of
society and the market,
we should consider "why has it disappeared?"
Also at that stage, "why was it not rational,
why was it not efficient?"

If we understand what has disappeared and
why it has disappeared
in the flow of rationalization and streamlining
in society and the market,
and understand what will revive,
then, finally, what should we consider?

We should consider "how can we revive them?"

This is step four.
We consider how we can revive
what disappeared in the flow of
rationalization and streamlining
by using recently developed technologies,
systems and institutions.

This is how to apply the law of spiral development.

A new medium
will emerge
intermediate between the "telephone" and "e-mail."

Concretely, what should we do?
Let us consider a practical exercise to apply the law.

For example, "e-mail."

There is no need to say this again, but
what has emerged in the flow of the rationalization and
streamlining of communication in society, is e-mail.

Certainly, through the popularization of e-mail,
our communication has become extremely convenient.
Because the telephone, which had been
our main means of communication until now,
had several disadvantages:

"We cut into the time of the addressee."
"We have to take notes with one hand."
"It is difficult to share information with a third party,
 since the information disappears on the spot."

These are the disadvantages.

In contrast,
e-mail has the following advantages:

"We can read it when we want to,
so we do not need to cut into the time of the addressee."
"We communicate by text,
so we do not need to take notes."
"It is easy to share information with a third party
by forwarding the mail."

And, above all else,
it has the advantage of "low-cost,"
thus it was rapidly popularized
in place of the telephone.

In this way, e-mail, which has now become the mainstream,
is certainly a more rational and efficient means
in comparison with the telephone.
But if we look closely at changes in
our communication patterns by the emergence of e-mail,
we notice that
the advantages the telephone had are disappearing
because of the popularization of e-mail.

Then, what has disappeared?

The "nuances of messages."

By replacement of the telephone with e-mail,
it has become difficult to convey
the nuances of messages.

Further spiral development
will occur with the telephone as
a means of communication.

That is, since the telephone is a means of communication
by voice, it can convey the emotion of the voice,
and so it could communicate delicate nuances.

Meanwhile, since e-mail is communication by text,
it cannot convey the emotion of the voice,
and therefore,
it has the disadvantage of being difficult to communicate
such delicate nuances.

Certainly through the emergence of e-mail,
communication has become convenient,
but the advantage that the telephone had
in being able to convey the emotion of the voice
has disappeared.

So what we should now consider is how we can revive
these "disappeared advantages"
through new technologies and methods.

For example, then, another technology of communication
intermediate between the telephone and e-mail
may revive, which has evolved to new functions.

That is "voice mail."

This technology and service already exists on the market.
But with the spread of broadband,
increase in capacity of portable terminals,
and a shift in business style,
"voice mail with a new function" may emerge.
If the new function voice mail spreads in the future,
there would be a revival of
"communication by voice" as in the period
when the telephone reigned supreme, and this is
a further manifestation of spiral development
in the means of communication.

However, this regression to the origin
is accompanied by the evolution to the future.
This "new function voice mail"
will have the following advantages:

"We can listen to it when we want to,
so we do not cut into the time of the addressee."
"Since a record remains of the voice,
we do not need to take notes on the spot."
"It is easy to share information with a third party,
by forwarding the file of voice."

For this reason, it will become a means of communication
that inherits the advantages of e-mail,
and overcomes the disadvantages of the telephone.

Of course, voice mail differs from the telephone,
since real-time conversation is not possible.
Also, there is a psychological resistance to
"leaving a voice recording behind."
Therefore, the evolution of such a means of communication
will continue while overcoming and getting around
these problems at times.

Chapter Two

Current "Trends"

Always "Reverse" Themselves in the Future.

The Second Law

The Law of Development through

"Negation of Negation."

Current "trends"
always "reverse" themselves
in the future.

In this way, the things around us go on
to achieve spiral development.
Let us look at the appearance of this development
from a slightly different viewpoint.

Not from the viewpoint of "function"
but from the viewpoint of "trend."

First, when we look at this spiral development
from the viewpoint of function,
it looks as if a function that had disappeared
has revived.
Then, if we view it from the viewpoint of trend,
what do we see?

A "reversal."

It looks
as if a reversal has happened to the previous trend.
That is, the trend of changes up to this point
now goes in an opposite direction.

In other words, this is a "rebound" of a trend.

If we consider trends in changes in the world,
they necessarily cause rebounds
in the opposite direction.

Just as a ball thrown against a wall jumps back
after hitting the wall, a "rebound" takes place.

Actually, there is another "law" in dialectic
that teaches us this.

It is
**the law of development through
"negation of negation."**

That is,

**Current "trends"
always "reverse" themselves in the future.**

That is the law.
To state this more simply,
things develop by two occurrences of negation.

That is, at first, some things begin to change
by being "negated,"
and at their end point,
that negation is negated once more,
and a new development arises.

However, the negation we are talking about here
is not a "mechanical negation"
but a "dialectical negation."
It never has the sense of
"erasing" or "destroying,"
rather it "exceeds," or "transcends" that stage.

Competition in "low-cost services"
always rebounds in the direction of
competition in "knowledge services."

Now, let us examine one example of this.

It is "online trading."

This is a service which makes it possible to trade in stocks
using the Internet, and it is clear why
this business model emerged and expanded so dramatically.

Because the trading fees in
the business model of conventional stockbrokerage firms
were too expensive.

Then, why were these fees expensive?

Because in conventional stockbrokerage firms,
the focus of service was "face-to-face" meeting by
contact persons or salespersons.

That is, the business model of "face-to-face" meetings that
not only offered "transaction services" for stock trading
but also offered "information services" such as
the latest trends in the market
and advice on stock trading.
For this reason, operating costs were high,
as were trading fees.

In contrast to this, the Internet stockbrokerage firms,
which offered online trading services,
had abandoned the conventional brokerage practice of
face-to-face information services.
And because they restricted it to
transaction services of stock trading over the Internet,
the operating costs were very low, and they could also
sharply reduce the trading fees.

This is the main reason why
the Net brokerages expanded so rapidly.

In a sense, this means that
the Net brokerages grew rapidly
because they negated the competition for
the conventional "face-to-face information services"
and engaged strictly in the competition
for "low-cost trading services."

This is the first "negation."

However, in this field of online trading,
numerous companies began to participate
in a very short period of time,
a large number of the Net brokerages appeared,
and "price wars" intensified.
For this reason, trading fees
had reached their lowest point.

It was a condition of so-called "price collapse."

And, what happened in this condition was
precisely the "rebound."

**At some stage,
"price competition" always reverses to
"value-added competition."**

Because in the midst of this "price competition"
surging to its limit,
many the Net brokerages began shifting their strategies.

They began to move their main battlefield
from "price competition" involving competing for
low-cost trading services
to "value-added competition" involving competing for
advanced information and knowledge services.

That is,
the "rationalization" and "streamlining" of online trading
advanced to their limits,
and at the stage where price competition
based on cost reduction reached its limit,
a reversal occurred.
That is, a rebound occurred.

This is the second "negation."

The price competition that began earlier in the form of
negating information service competition
underwent a "reversal" in the direction towards
information service competition
now in the form of negating price competition.

This is an example of the law of
development through "negation of negation."

Of course, this newly emerging information service
resulting from "negation of negation" was not
a revival of an earlier "face-to-face information service."
It had evolved by ascending one more step
on the spiral staircase.

The "information and knowledge services"
at this new stage has become much more "convenient"
for the customer, by utilizing the Internet or broadband,
at the point of rapidity, accuracy, comprehensiveness,
searchability, and bidirectionality.

And this "development through negation of negation"
is not occurring only in the field of online trading.
From now on, it will occur in other domains as well.

First, in some domains, an all-out price competition
will begin by negating the ways of the existing
inefficient, highly priced services.
But when the price competition reaches its limit,
it will shift to value-added competition of services
by negating the price competition.

For example, for the customer, this will involve
"knowledge services" offering rich knowledge and wisdom,
"mind services" offering warmth and
consideration and "one-to-one services"
with full consideration of the customer.

Value-added competition based on
offering such services will begin.
And such a reversal through "negation of negation"
will become a phenomenon to be always witnessed in
many domains of business
where rationalization is progressing.

**In the "knowledge society,"
"knowledge expressible in words" will lose its value and
"wisdom inexpressible in words" will acquire value.**

Now, let us look at one more example of
this reversal and rebound.

It is the paradox of the "knowledge society."

If we ask, "what kind of society
will we have from now on?"
many people will answer this with
a "knowledge society."

"If so, what kind of society will this be?"
In answer to this question, surely many people
will reply a "society in which knowledge has value."

But in reality, a knowledge society
is a "society in which knowledge loses its value."

Because this knowledge society,
if we look at it in greater depth,
will appear to develop spirally.

First, in society prior to the knowledge society,
the media had not developed much,
so ordinary people could not easily acquire
specialist knowledge or recent knowledge.
Therefore, these types of knowledge carried a high value.

However, with the advent of the Net revolution,
many people acquired information terminals such as
cell phones and personal computers,
and communication costs dropped dramatically.
Moreover, every day, enormous amounts of information
were made public on websites,
and countless knowledge communities
were born on the Internet.

For that reason, in the new coming age,
"knowledge expressible in words" itself will be
available to everyone without time, effort and cost.
So the knowledge expressible in words
representing specialist knowledge or recent knowledge
ends up losing its relative value.

This means that
a "society in which knowledge has lost its value."

Then, if knowledge expressible in words
is losing its value, what is coming to have value?

"Wisdom inexpressible in words."

For example, wisdom inexpressible in words
such as skills, senses, techniques and know-how,
will come to have great value
in the knowledge society that is emerging.

This precisely
is spiral development of the knowledge society.

The "age of knowledge"
is ending
and the "age of wisdom" is beginning.

This is because in earlier societies,
wisdom inexpressible in words had great value.

For example, in the workplace for apprentices,
as expressed by the words "learn with your body,"
"grasp it with your breath,"
the "wisdom" of skills, senses, techniques and know-how
had great value.
Such wisdom could not be expressed by words,
and they were things that were impossible
to communicate or acquire easily.

However, through the invention of printing technology,
mass media was born.
This mass media, which made it possible to
communicate knowledge expressible in words
to many people, enabled them to share and utilize
specialist knowledge and recent knowledge.
And in this way, mass media improved
the productivity of society as a whole,
created a rich culture
and promoted the development of society.

However, even at this stage, in order to learn
"knowledge," people needed "schools,"
which restricted them in place and time,
or "books," which needed cost and time for distribution.

For this reason, knowledge expressible in words
had a high value in society at that stage.

But then, the Net revolution occurred.

This revolution realized a personal media
that surpasses mass media, and anyone,
as long as they had an information terminal,
could easily acquire
specialist knowledge and recent knowledge.

As a result, knowledge expressible in words lost
its relative value, and in a new dimension,
wisdom inexpressible in words
again acquired great value.

In this way, if we look back on history up to the time of
the knowledge society, the earlier "age of wisdom"
developed into the "age of knowledge."
But, since sharing of knowledge became easier
through the Net revolution,
a reversal and rebound occurred,
then the age of knowledge is moving in the direction of
an age of wisdom in a new dimension now.

This is also an example of
"development through negation of negation."

The trend towards "high-tech"
necessarily
rebounds towards "high-touch."

In this way, when we look at the world,
we notice that this law of
"development through negation of negation"
is happening universally.

This trend very much resembles
the movement of a "pendulum."

The world seems to change
in the same way as a pendulum.

That is, when the world changes in a certain direction,
when it reaches its end point,
it begins to move in the opposite direction.
And when we understand this,
we can acquire a "macro view."

For example, in which direction is
"high-tech society" moving?

It is clear, if we consider this pendulum.

The trend towards "high-tech," at its end point,
will necessarily move in the direction of "high-touch."

This is what we will notice.

Societies that are pursuing high-tech by
leveraging the leading edge science and technology,
at its end point, will necessarily move
in the direction of a society which highly values
high-touch, that is, care and concern for people.

For example, this is quite clear if we examine
the successful cases of advanced the "Net shops" in Japan.

In the beginning,
in order to make the Net shops successful,
high-tech was considered to play a key role, such as
the introduction of electronic transaction systems,
clear displays of product images, and
development of product databases.
However, when we view the development of
the Net shops that followed this,
most of the successful shops
naturally had introduced high-tech,
but they made use of e-mail, and customer communities,
creating establishments that greatly valued
high-touch with their customers.

In this way, by pursuing high-tech, at its end point,
the pendulum necessarily begins to move
in the direction of high-touch.

And, in the background of this trend,
there are two laws of dialectic such as
the law of development through "spiral process" and
the law of development through "negation of negation."

We should understand this.

The "dialectic worldview"
existed
also in ancient Eastern philosophy.

However, as we mentioned in the foreword,
this dialectic was by no means
an "original idea" of Hegel's philosophy or of
Western philosophy.

Actually, this "dialectic worldview" existed
also in Eastern philosophy since long ago.

For example, the following words in Taoism
teach us that:

"Yang ultimately is Yin."
"Yin ultimately is Yang."

These words in Taoism mean that
changes in things, at their end point,
undergo reversal.
And Eastern philosophy had discerned
this fact since long ago.

Also, this law of dialectic
is related in various words
in Eastern philosophy.

For example, there are the words:

"The Great Self (*"Taiga"*) resembles
the Non Self (*"Muga"*)."

When the hearts of human beings
move in the direction of realizing
the great ideal called *"Taiga"* (the Great Self),
strangely, they approach
the boundaries of *"Muga"* (the Non Self).
That is what these words teach us.

Also, when human beings age, becoming elderly,
for some reason, they return to the world of innocence
and ingenuousness, like an infant.
The famous Japanese Zen master Ryokan,
undertook severe disciplinary training from a young age,
and reached a deep state of being.
In his old age, as legends have it,
he was moving in the direction of playing innocently
with little children, and having a good time.

Also, in Japan where everything is considered as
a "path" to the world of the spirit of Zen.
Even in the world of fishing,
we can speak deeply of the "Tao of fishing."
And in this world there is the saying:

"Fishing begins with carp, and fishing ends with carp."

This is also none other than the words suggesting
"spiral development."

If we look carefully, we can see that the world of
Eastern philosophy abounds in the laws of dialectic.

**When we apply dialectic thinking,
we can foresee the next "main battlefield"
and it serves us in "strategic thinking."**

Up to this point we have been discussing
two laws of dialectic:
the law of development through "spiral process" and
the law of development through "negation of negation."

When understanding this, the readers
naturally harbor one new question in their mind.

> Then, how can we take advantage of these laws
> in implementing actual change?

That is the question.

At this point, let us discuss just how we can
implement these laws in "strategic thinking."

Until now, we have discussed how important it is
to foresee the revival of functions which had disappeared
as well as the reversal in current trends, by applying
the law of development through "spiral process" and
the law of development through "negation of negation."

What does it mean, from the viewpoint of
strategic thinking, to foresee these
revivals and reversals?

Foreseeing the next "main battlefield."

For example, by discerning
the spiral development in society and the market,
foreseeing what will revive
and what direction will they reverse to from now on
is to discern the next direction of competition
between nations and between companies.
It is also to discern where
the current main battlefield will shift next.

As mentioned earlier, in the ages before the "dog year,"
changes in the world were unhurried,
as was the shift to a new main battlefield.
Consequently, in strategic thinking for nations
and companies, there was no need to be concerned
where the next main battlefield would be.
It was sufficient to consider only the strategies
for the current main battlefield.

However, in the age of the "dog year" from now,
changes in the world are stormy,
and shifts in the main battlefields are very rapid,
so in strategic thinking, we must constantly be concerned
about where the next main battlefield will be.
Without considering
what will be the next main battlefield,
we cannot formulate a strategy.

In order to consider this,
let us discuss an important example.

It is an insight into the direction which
the main battlefield of market competition
will move into because of the Net revolution.

The Internet revolution triggers
not only a simple "rationalization of the market"
but also the "evolution of the market."

Now, when asked
"what will happen because of the Internet revolution?"
executives will unanimously reply
with the words:

"Rationalization," "streamlining" and "cost reduction."

That is, many executives today believe that
the essence of the Net revolution is rationalization
and streamlining of company, markets and society
and cost reductions through them.

However, this belief is unfortunately in error.
The essence of the Net revolution
is not such a rationalization.

Then, what is it?

It is "evolution."

For example, what happens through the Net revolution is
not just the "rationalization of the market"
in the sense that market transactions become rapid
and accurate at low cost.

What happens through the Net revolution is
that the nature of the market itself undergoes
a fundamental change; one that should be called
"evolution of the market."

Then, what is this evolution of the market?

An evolution from the "company-centric market"
to the "customer-centric market."

That is,
most of the business models in the markets until now
were constructed as company-centric.
But as a result of the Net revolution,
all of the business models
will be transformed into customer-centric ones.

For example, the auction and reverse auction
that we have described earlier.

It is the business model in which the prices of products,
which have been determined by the company side until now,
are determined by the customer side.

Also the Net-based group purchase model.
From the viewpoint of the customer,
this is a business model in which
the "customers" gather, raise their voices
and demand "discounts" from the company.

And the essence of the Net revolution is
the evolution of the market as a whole
from company-centric to customer-centric
through recombinations of such business models.

In the customer-centric market
an evolution of the middleman will occur
through spiral development.

Now, what will happen in this evolved
customer-centric market?

A dialectic spiral development will occur.
As will an evolution through "negation of negation."

To state it concretely, what will be the evolution?

"Evolution of the middleman."

In the markets, the middleman,
through a dialectic process,
will evolve from an old middleman to a new middleman.

What kind of process is this?

Just about when the Net revolution began in the US,
many people replied as follows to the question
"what will now happen to the markets?"

"The middleman will die."

Actually because of the Net revolution,
"disintermediation" occurred, in which
those middlemen were bypassed, who conventionally
did retailing and wholesaling, because it became easy
for producers to sell directly to consumers.
And many middlemen were selected out.

However, in this customer-centric market,
within a few years,
something happened that most people had not anticipated.
Several years after the Net revolution occurred,
people began saying:

"The middleman never dies."

That is because the middleman revived in the market.
But, this was not the old-fashioned type of middleman.
Rather, an entirely new type of middleman appeared,
called the "new middleman."

Then, what is the difference between
the "old middleman" and the "new middleman?"

The direction that they face is different.
The conventional middleman
such as a retailer and a wholesaler
faced towards the company and
engaged in a business model based on "sales agent,"
while the new middleman faces towards the customer
and engages in a business model based on
"purchasing agent."

Now most of the companies called
the Net businesses actually follow
the business model of the new middleman.

The "middleman" who once was negated will come back in the form of the new middleman.

For example, Amazon.com, which grew rapidly
in the world of the Net business,
is not only a company functioning
as a sales agent for books over the Internet.
Actually this company serves to offer
a purchasing agent to the reader.

This is because the Amazon sites,
responding to the needs of the readers,
offer many services as follows:

Confirming of availability and time of delivery.
Searching for used books.
Auctioning of non-needed items.
Introducing related books.
Providing of reviews of books.

And this is the new middleman,
who offers comprehensive services of
both the "purchasing agent" and the "purchasing support"
in order to make available to the readers
what they are seeking.

And if we examine
the essence of this company,
we see that not only Amazon
but most the Net businesses actually follow this
new middleman business model.

And the Net revolution thus has brought about
the evolution from the old middleman
to the new middleman in the market.
This process of the evolution of the middleman
is also the process of
"development through negation of negation" of dialectic.

That is, in the very beginning, in the flow of
rationalization through the Net revolution
the "disintermediation" occurred.
As the words of "the old middleman will die" suggests,
the old middleman was selected out
and was negated.

However, soon in the markets,
along with the words "the middleman never dies,"
the middleman, who was negated,
has revived.

The middleman has revived
as a new occupation called the new middleman.

Certainly, this is the process of
"development through negation of negation."

The once negated middleman
has revived as the new middleman
through "negation of negation."

**By using dialectic thinking,
we can adopt the "strategy of preemption"
by foreseeing the "revival" and "reversal."**

This is the evolution of the middleman
in the customer-centric market.

And if we gain an insight into
the "next evolution" of this middleman,
we can see the "next main battlefield" clearly.

It is the battlefield that involves
the position of the new middleman.

That is, in the customer-centric market,
the new middleman, who is offering such services as
"purchasing agent" and "purchasing support"
from the standpoint of the customer,
will quite naturally gather strong empathy
from the customer and seize leadership in the market.

Consequently, in each market
competition will begin centered on
the position of the new middleman
having the most trust from the customers.

Who will become
the first new middleman in that market?
Who will become
the strongest new middleman in that market?
Which new middleman should we tie up with?

Competition will start from
the consideration of these issues.

So if we understand deeply
the law of "spiral development" and
the law of "negation of negation,"

And if we gain an insight into
the answers to the following questions:

In the markets from now on,
what will revive?
In which direction will reversals occur?
Where will the main battlefield move towards next?

Then, we can naturally decide the strategy to take.

Now, at such a time, what kind of strategy do we need?

The "strategy of preemption."

What should we do if we figure out
where the main battlefield will move towards next?

We should preempt to that next main battlefield
and establish a strategic beachhead earlier than others.

For example, if we gain an insight into
the evolution of the middleman,
we should begin the business model of the new middleman
ahead of others in that market.
We should emerge as the first new middleman in that market.

This is the strategy of preemption.

**In the age of the "dog year"
strategic thinking evolves
because the "strategic wait time" is reduced.**

And in this age of the "dog year,"
this strategy of preemption will become
extremely effective.

Why is this?

Because the "wait time" is short.

In the age of the "dog year,"
the wait time to move into
the next main battlefield is short.

Conversely, in ages prior to the "dog year,"
even if we adopted a strategy of preemption,
market changes were slow-paced,
so the "strategic wait time" became too long.
For this reason, it exceeded the "strategic endurance time"
determined by the relationship of
the financial and organizational ability of the company,
in many cases,
resulting in their "inability to wait any longer."

But from now we will have the age of the "mouse year,"
which surpasses the "dog year."
And the main battlefield in the market
will shift very rapidly.

Therefore, even if we foresee
the "next main battlefield," it is late.
Sometimes we must even foresee
the "one after the next main battlefield."

So, the shift of the main battlefield
from the old middleman to the new middleman.
Where will the next main battlefield be after?

We shall discuss an insight here.

The new middleman will evolve further
into the "concierge."

Consequently, in markets where there are already
many business models of the new middleman,
it will become desirable to adopt
the strategy of preemption
aiming at evolving into
the "concierge" business model.

Then, what is this "concierge?"

It is a new extended customer-centric business model
that goes beyond purchasing agent and purchasing support
to offer services of
"lifestyle support" and "lifestyle advice."

In the Net business, now
this new main battlefield is coming into view.

Chapter Three

When the "Quantity"

Exceeds a Specific Level,

The "Quality" Changes Dramatically.

The Third Law

The Law of Development through

"Transformation from Quantity to Quality."

When the "quantity"
exceeds a specific level,
the "quality" changes dramatically.

In this way, by applying two laws of dialectic,
the law of development through "spiral process" and
the law of development through "negation of negation,"
we can foresee the next main battlefield.
We can foresee
where the "main battlefield" will move to.

However, when described in this way,
another question may arise in the reader's mind.

Then, when does the main battlefield shift?

Put in another way,
in dialectic development, the questions are as follows:
When does the "revival" of nostalgic things occur?
When does the "reversal" of current trends begin?

Unfortunately, however, there is no method
for predicting clearly the period in which
this "shift of the main battlefield" will occur.
There is no method for predicting concretely
the period when
"the main battlefield will shift."

But, there is a method for judging
the "possibility" of the shift occurring.

Actually, in dialectic,
there is one more law that teaches us this.
What is it?

It is
**the law of development through
"transformation from quantity to quality."**

That is,

**When the "quantity" exceeds a specific level,
the "quality" changes dramatically.**

That is the law.

Then, what is an example of this law?
The most familiar example
is the "evaporation of water."

When we put water in a kettle, and
apply heat from below, the temperature rises gradually.
And when the water temperature reaches 100 degrees,
the water changes to steam, bubbles form,
and evaporation begins.

This is a phenomenon by which,
when the "quantity" called water temperature
increases, and exceeds 100 degrees,
the "quality" changes from liquid to gas.

When "shares"
exceed a specific level,
a "de facto standard" naturally emerges.

The "evaporation of water" is an example in the natural world,
but there are many examples of this
also in society and the market.

For example, when new products with different technical
standards generate intense competition in the market,
one of them occupies the dominant position in share,
and the shares exceed a specific level,
many customers, at an accelerated pace,
start buying the product.
And as a result the standard of that product
becomes the "de facto standard"
and it dominates the market.

This phenomenon also means that
the increase in the quantity of this "share"
brings about a change in its quality,
in the form of a "standard" or "monopoly."

In this way,
most things in the world have a property that
when their quantity exceeds a specific level,
either instantly or rapidly,
their quality will undergo a major change.

This is because, in the background of the phenomena
called "discontinuous change" and "evolution,"
exists the "law of transformation
from quantity to quality" of dialectic.

Let us take one more important example.
It is the case of the "new middleman" mentioned earlier.

When hearing about this discussion of
the new middleman,
the reader most likely harbors one question.

Why has the new middleman appeared at this time?

That is the question.

The answer is clear as follows:

The services called
"purchasing agent" and "purchasing support"
which the new middleman offers.
The customer needs for such services existed from the past.

This is not the service of a "sales agent"
who promotes the sale of products
from the standpoint of the company,
but the service of a "purchasing agent"
who supports the purchase of products
from the standpoint of the customer.

The customer needs for this service
have existed from the past.

Since long before the birth of the new middleman,
this is, for customers, the most desirable service and
a service which was in very strong demand.

But, it was extremely difficult to provide this service.

Why was that?

When there is a dramatic drop
in "cost,"
the "business model" evolves.

Because the cost was too high.

That is, no matter how much
the service was needed by the customer,
the service of purchasing agent and purchasing support
by the new middleman
cost too much to be realized.

Gathering and offering information on every product
related to the special needs of the customer.
Acting all the procedure for the purchase
on behalf of the customer.

If we attempted to offer such service in business,
enormous costs would be incurred.
So, it was impossible to realize,
considering the cost burden to the customer.

That is, a great "cost barrier" existed.

This is the most important reason that
the new middleman did not appear in the market
despite the strong needs of the customer.

In other words, the excessive communication costs
to provide the information the customer needed
was the major reason why it would not work.

However, a "revolution" occurred.

The Net revolution broke down this cost barrier.

This is because the Internet could cut
the communication costs for providing information
from company to customer
down to 1000th of the cost before the Internet.
Actually,
in the present age of the broadband Internet,
the cost has probably come down even more.

That is why the new middleman appeared.

By using portal sites and e-mail,
the communication costs to the customer
dropped dramatically.

For this reason, the service of
"purchasing agent" or "purchasing support,"
which had been impossible owing to excessive costs,
became possible to realize,
and many new middlemen appeared in the market.

Then, what does it mean?

The "quantitative" change,
which was the dramatic drop in
communication costs,
brought about the "qualitative" change,
which was the evolution from the old middleman
to the new middleman.

When cost drops dramatically, the consciousness of the consumer changes greatly.

This is the law of development through
"transformation from quantity to quality."

Now, when considering
the "time to shift the main battlefield" in the market,
it is extremely useful to know this law.

When discerning changes in the market,
and foreseeing where the main battlefield will shift to,
it helps us understand
"what indices" to focus on and
"what quantities" to pay attention to.

For example, the "broadband revolution,"
a new stage in the Net revolution.

How will this broadband revolution
change the quality of the market
in the future?
In order to discern this,
what indices should we pay attention to?

Many experts focus on the quantity of
"distribution of digital contents,"
especially, the distribution of music and movies.
Because many experts predict that
as broadband becomes popular,
many people will be able to listen to music
and watch movies freely, by using the Internet.

And because they predict also that
a great quantity of digital contents must be distributed
in order to realize that.

Of course, owing to the broadband revolution,
the circulation of music and movies
will become very large in quantity.
However, the most important thing that
the broadband revolution will actually change
is not this "circulation of digital contents."

Then, what is it?

It is the "consciousness of people."

This is because the broadband revolution has realized
a "dramatic drop in the Internet connection fees."

Through the broadband revolution,
"continuous connection" and "unlimited access"
became possible.

For this reason, the people
who had been using the Internet
mindful of connection fees,
are now able to use the Internet as they wish,
without worrying about cost.

And this has changed
the "consciousness of people" greatly.

When the "consciousness of the consumer" changes greatly, the market evolves into a "customer-centric market."

For example, when purchasing a product,
it has become a trend to purchase
by making thorough comparisons of products
by accessing lots of information easily
by using the Internet.

Also, it has become a trend to purchase products
by listening to the opinions of friends or acquaintances
and listening to the voices of other consumers
on the Net community.

Thus the consciousness of people changed greatly.

That is, the services of continuous connection
and unlimited access, which were considered
to be minor changes in the broadband revolution,
fundamentally altered the consciousness of people
towards information.

This also is the law of development through
"transformation from quantity to quality."

The quantitative change in the "Internet connection fees"
brought about the qualitative change in
the "consciousness of people."

In this way, the curtain will finally rise
when the consciousness of people has changed
through this revolution.

A full-fledged "customer-centric market."

The curtain has finally risen on this market.

The curtain of the customer-centric market
will rise not only because in the market
many "customer-centric business models" will spread
and a number of new middlemen will appear.

The great number of customers and citizens.

When the consciousness of these people towards
"information" will change fundamentally, finally
the curtain of the true customer-centric market will rise.

And, at this time,
the market will enter the real stage of "evolution."

That is, the "evolution of the market"
does not mean simply
the evolution of the "business model" or
the evolution of the "middleman."

The evolution of
the "consciousness of the consumer" in the market.
The evolution of
the "consciousness of the people" in society.

This is precisely what is meant by
the "evolution of the market" and
the "evolution of society."

**By dramatically dropping costs,
we can accelerate
the "shift of the main battlefield."**

What is the law of development through
"transformation from quantity to quality?"
How do we implement this law strategically?

Up to now, from these viewpoints,
we have discussed the following two items:

How do we foresee
in what direction the main battlefield will shift?
And when will this main battlefield shift?

However, one question will most likely arise
in the mind of the reader who hears such statements.

Then, how can we accelerate
the shift of that main battlefield?

Certainly, this is an important question.

If we are able to foresee in what direction
the main battlefield will move,
we can establish a strategic beachhead
for this battlefield through "preemption."
And we can wait for this main battlefield to come.
We have discussed
the importance of the strategy of preemption.

However, if we take this strategy of preemption,
the next question we must face is
"how can we
accelerate the shift of the main battlefield?"

For example, let us consider the above cases.
If, based on the insight mentioned above,
we want to accelerate the arrival of
the "customer-centric market"
through the broadband revolution, what must we do?

We must
"spread the customer-centric business model."
We must "foster new middlemen in markets."

These strategic measures are important,
but if we are in the communication industry,
it is clear what the most important measure is.

We must "bring down communication fees."

We need to accelerate this.
By doing this, the "transformation
from quantity to quality" will necessarily occur.
And at some stage,
the consciousness of people towards information
will necessarily begin to change greatly.
And at that time,
the market will evolve into a customer-centric market,
not only at the level of
a business model or a middleman,
but also at the level of "market culture."

That is, the quantitative change in connection fees
will bring about the qualitative change in market culture.

**By dramatically increasing
the "number of users,"
we can promote the evolution of the market.**

In this way, in order to accelerate
the "transformation from quantity to quality"
in the market,
the strategy of dropping the price of a product
below a specific level
has become an important strategy.

And such a strategy of acceleration by
the transformation from quantity to quality
has actually been used sometimes in the past.

For example,
when promoting a new product in the market,
there are some cases where
the strategic objective of development and sales
is set to offer a product at an inexpensive price
which is lower than a specific price level.

It is well known that the popularity
was suddenly accelerated for products such as
DVD recorders and large screen TVs,
at the stage where the prices
dropped below a specific level.

Consequently, when accelerating
the transformation from quantity to quality
in the market,
we sometimes need to focus on the "quantity,"
that is, the price of a product.

However, in the age of the Net revolution,
in order to accelerate the evolution of the market,
there is one other important "quantity"
that we need to focus on.

What is that?

The "number of users."

In order to accelerate the "evolution of the market"
in the age of the Net revolution,
not only the "price of a product,"
but also the index called the "number of users"
becomes extremely important.

If we consider the essence of the network society,
this is only natural.

For example, telephones became convenient
because many people owned them.
If only a single individual owned a telephone,
it would have no value.
And, even if only a few people had them,
the range of their utility would be limited.
This is as true with the fax as with e-mail.

In this way, most of the technologies, products
and services in the network society are useful
because they are used by many people.
This is called the "network effect."

When the "number of users"
exceeds a specific level,
self acceleration begins.

Conversely,
the technologies, products, and services
in the network society
become useful to everyone,
as the number of people who use them increases.
Then more and more people
will begin to use them.

This means, in the words of the leading edge science,
namely the "science of complex systems,"
that the technologies, products and services
in the network society
now have the property of "self acceleration."
And for this reason, in the network society,
the number of users is an important index.

When the number of users increases
and exceeds a specific level,
at that point, self acceleration begins
and the nature of society and market begins
to change rapidly and on a large scale.

A well-known example
in which this fact was used strategically
is the strategy taken by Netscape Communications, Inc.
at the beginning of the Net revolution.

By spreading the revolutionary software,
"Netscape Navigator," Netscape took the initiative
to raise the curtain of the Net revolution.
At the beginning it adopted the strategy of
distributing the software free of charge to everyone.
It was a strategy based on the idea that
the more the number of users increases,
the greater the value of the Internet browser becomes.

This strategy of "free distribution"
later brought about the success of many products
and it is no longer very unusual.
If we survey the world around us,
we will find many businesses in which
markets suddenly launch and develop
as the number of users exceeds a specific level.

For example, in recent years,
we have seen a rapid expansion of blogs.
Since it is attractive for bloggers
to connect with each other
through track back and commenting,
the more the number of users increased,
the greater the merits became.
So, at a certain stage
they expanded explosively.

Consequently,
the strategy to rapidly increase the "number of users"
by venturing to implement
the free distribution of products
is also a strategy for accelerating
the shift of the "main battlefield"
and an effective measure for accelerating
the "transformation from quantity to quality."

The transformation from "quantity" to "quality" begins when "buzzwords" are forgotten.

Now, how can we judge whether or not
a "quantity" has exceeded a specific level as an index?

There is no absolute method for this,
but there is one "indicator" which can be of some help.

Whether or not a "buzzword"
has been forgotten.

This is an "indicator."

Let us discuss a familiar example.
There are such items as the "telephone," the "fax,"
the "Internet" and "e-mail."
At the time when these new technologies,
products and services in the network societies,
first emerge on the scene and expand throughout society,
these "buzzwords" attract attention and appear with great
frequency in the mass media.

However, when they had spread throughout society
as a whole, and penetrated it,
these "buzzwords" actually began to disappear.

For example, in the past when the Net revolution
had just begun,
the word "Internet" frequently appeared in the mass media,
and many people used it as a cool, cutting edge buzzword.

However, now that the Internet has spread and penetrated
into all corners of society,
for example, people who use cell phones to
get information from the websites,
are no longer consciously thinking
"well I guess I will use the Internet
to get some information."
They have even forgotten that they are using
the Internet terminals for that purpose.

That is, when we begin to forget that the technologies,
products and services are close at hand,
they have, in fact, adequately spread
throughout society and have penetrated it.

For example, let us think about the hybrid automobile,
which is now popular as an environment-friendly car.
As long as people are conscious of the fact
that "they are driving a hybrid car,"
we cannot say that it has reached
its substantial popularity.
We can say that only after
it has faded from the consciousness of the people.

Consequently,
whether or not the "buzzword" has been forgotten.

That is one indicator.

It is only when it has been forgotten
that it has really begun to happen.

The "transformation from quantity to quality"
has begun to happen quietly and profoundly in society.

Chapter Four

Things Which Oppose and

Compete with Each Other

Come to Resemble Each Other.

The Fourth Law

The Law of Development through

"Interpenetration of Opposing Objects."

Things which oppose and compete with each other come to resemble each other.

Now, when gaining an insight into
the essence of changes in the world
and foreseeing the future,
there is one other important law in dialectic,
in addition to the following laws:

The law of development through "spiral process."
The law of development through "negation of negation."
The law of development through
"transformation from quantity to quality."

It is
**the law of development through
"interpenetration of opposing objects."**

That is,

**Things which oppose and compete with each other
come to resemble each other.**

That is the law.

Let us discuss this law in terms of
two laws we have already described.

First, the law of development through "spiral process"
is the law in which
old things revive as if climbing a spiral staircase.
From another viewpoint, this means that
old things revive with involving new things
and new things develop with involving old things.

Also
the law of development through "negation of negation"
is the law in which things once negated
return to their origins through being negated again.
From another viewpoint, it means that
new things that negate old things
return with old things negated.

That is, in dialectic, two things which appear to
oppose and compete each other,
such as old things and new things,
things to negate and things to be negated,
come to involve each other, and as a result,
both of them "merge" and become "integrated."

That is the law of development through
"interpenetration of opposing objects."

The "Real business" and
the "Net business"
will necessarily merge.

Let us take a concrete example.

At the beginning of the Net revolution
the phrase "Real versus Net" was often used.

This was a debate over which type of business was
superior, and advantageous in competition
between the "Real businesses" on the street and
the "Net businesses" having electronic shops
on the Internet.

But, this phrase was soon replaced by
the phrase "click and mortar."

That is, people started to recognize that
it was important in businesses
to combine successfully the Net business of "click"
and the Real business of "mortar" and
to develop them strategically.

However, at present, phrases like
"Real versus Net" and "click and mortar"
are no longer used.

This is because, in all businesses
the Real businesses and the Net businesses have merged.
Because they have integrated with each other.

These days, there is no Real business without
considering using the Internet.

At present, many companies and shops
have their own websites and homepages on the Internet
in addition to their Real shops.
And they are in the practice of taking orders
through their websites and e-mail.

On the other hand, now there is no Net business
without considering having Real operations.
At the beginning of the Net revolution,
during the Christmas rush in the United States,
many the Net businesses that were selling products
faced the problem of late delivery,
and they were greatly criticized for this.
Today, naturally the Net businesses are facing
the necessity to consider carefully combining
Real operations such as services of shop inventory control,
delivery service, telephone communications
and in-store product explanations.

In this way, the Real business and the early Net business
were described as opposing each other,
symbolized by the phrase "Real versus Net."
Now, however, these businesses have learned
from each other, have undergone interpenetration,
and the business model that has merged the two
has become both common practice and mainstream.

Thus, there are a large number of examples of
development through
"interpenetration of opposing objects"
in many areas of business.

Brokerage firms and banks
mutually
evolve into "universal banks."

For example, the interpenetration of
the conventional brokerages and the Net brokerages.
This is what is happening in the Japanese markets.

When the Net brokerages first appeared on the scene,
the conventional brokerages believed
that customers would not trade in
their important stocks by using the Internet.
But they were overwhelmed by
the rapid growth of the Net brokerages,
and as a result they rapidly started to provide
online trading services.

However, it is interesting that on the other hand,
the Net brokerages that had once rejected Real shops,
are now opening actual shops on the street
in order to enhance their points of contact with customers.
That is, they have started in-store services.

And, as a result of this interpenetration taking place,
at present, every brokerage
is becoming an "evolved brokerage"
which offers general services
by the merging of the Net and Real shops.

Similarly, in the banking world
the Internet banks appeared,
which offer services on the Internet,
without having physical locations.
And interpenetration occurred here also
through competition with conventional banks.
So at present, all banks have become "evolved banks"
by integrating the Net and the Real services.

Moreover, if we view this trend in the financial world
on a wider perspective, these brokerage firms
and banks are also undergoing interpenetration.

This interpenetration will occur as follows:
Brokerage firms concentrating on "direct financing"
and banks concentrating on "indirect financing"
were competing with each other, and fighting
over customers in the financial services area.
But through relaxation of regulations and liberalization
in the financial industry called the "financial Big Bang,"
banks will move into brokerage services, and
brokerage firms will move into banking.
In this way, interpenetration will occur.

As a result of such interpenetration, after all,
both brokerage firms and banks
will begin evolving in the direction of
general financial services called "universal banks."

This has already occurred in the financial industries
in Europe and the United States
and has also begun in Japan.

For-profit companies and non-profit organizations mutually evolve into "social enterprises."

However, such interpenetration
does not only occur within one industry, or
between different industries.
It happens also on a much larger scale.

For example, interpenetration occurs also between
for-profit companies and non-profit organizations.

This is because now two major trends
are emerging in the world.

The first is a trend towards
"corporate social responsibility" (CSR).

That is,
"social responsibility" and "social contributions"
are now being demanded of for-profit companies,
which had tended to consider their main mission
to pursue profit.
This stems from reflecting on
the numerous business scandals that
have occurred in various countries around the world.
That is, they are expected to act not only for
the profit of their own companies,
but also for
the benefit of society at large.

The second is a trend towards "social entrepreneurship."

For example,
non-profit organizations that have been conventionally
operated depending on benefactors contribution and
government supports are now expected to adopt
a style of "social entrepreneur," which
would raise their operating revenue properly through
entrepreneurial spirit and entrepreneurial methods,
thus securing the independence and
sustainability of their operations.

This is, in a sense, the interpenetration that
for-profit companies learned from non-profits
concerning "social contribution," and
non-profit organizations learned from for-profits
concerning "economic base."

Consequently, in the coming age, these two major trends of
corporate social responsibility and social entrepreneurship
will merge together.
As a result, a new form of business organization
called a "social enterprise," which goes beyond
the two opposing terms "for-profit" and "non-profit,"
will appear.

That is, this is a new form of business organization
which proclaims a clear objective of making contributions
to society through its main businesses,
and at the same time secures the profits for
the operation, sustainability and
development of the organization.

From now on, many for-profit companies and
non-profit organizations will very likely
evolve into this new form of business organization.

Capitalism and socialism
have evolved
through interpenetration.

This example of interpenetration
exists not only in the economic world,
but also in the political world.

For example, under two-party political institutions,
this interpenetration often takes place.

Because, under a two-party system,
opposing parties are strongly conscious of
the demands of the electorate and try to incorporate
the good parts of the policies of their opponents,
and as a result their policies end up
being not too different from each other.

For this kind of interpenetration of policies,
as symbolized by policy changes in
the Conservative and Labour Parties in the UK,
there are many other cases around the world.

And, such interpenetration
also occurs in the state and in social systems.

In the past there was an age in which
the "capitalist states" of America and Western Europe
and the "socialist states" of the USSR, Eastern Europe,
and China were opposing and in conflict with each other
as two social systems.

However, most of the capitalist states,
under the form of "principles of social democracy,"
adopted policies for fulfilling social welfare
and improving the rights of the workers.

In contrast, the former "socialist states" of
Russia and China adopted
capitalism and market principles into their state system.

These are also examples of interpenetration
at the levels of state and social systems,
that occurred in the course of history.

In this way,
the law of development through
"interpenetration of opposing objects" in dialectic
gives precious hints for gaining an insight into
the essence of what is currently taking place
in companies, markets, and societies,
foreseeing what will happen,
and determining new policies and strategies.

Things which oppose and compete with each other
come to resemble each other.

If we look around,
there are numerous examples of this law,
from cases of products, personnel, and companies,
to cases of markets, economies and societies,
and from everyday events to historical events.

Chapter Five

Contradiction is the Driving Force

For the Development of the World.

The Fifth Law

The Law of Development through

"Sublation of Contradiction."

Contradiction
is the driving force
for the development of the world.

So far, we have discussed
the following four laws of dialectic from the viewpoint of
"how can we foresee the future?":

The law of development through "spiral process."
The law of development through "negation of negation."
The law of development through
"transformation from quantity to quality."
The law of development through
"interpenetration of opposing objects."

However, at the roots of these four laws,
exists the most fundamental law.

Now, let us discuss this fundamental law.
What kind of law is it?

It is
the law of development through
"sublation of contradiction."

That is,

**Contradiction is the driving force
for the development of the world.**

That is the law.

To put it simply, this law means that:

All things contain within themselves "contradictions,"
but those very contradictions become
the "driving forces" of their development.
And when such contradictions are not
"resolved" mechanically
but sublated dialectically,
their development is achieved.

In a sense,
this is the most important law underlying dialectic.
And this law represents the most basic idea of dialectic.

That is, things in the world change, develop, and evolve
because contradictions exist in those things.

And those very contradictions are
the driving forces of their development
and are none other than the "life forces" that
cause things to change, develop, and evolve.

This is the idea underlying dialectic.

And for this reason,
dialectic is called the "philosophy of contradiction."

The essence of
management is
the "management of contradiction."

Let us take a concrete example.

The contradiction between
"pursuit of profit" and "social contribution"
in managing a company.

When involved in managing a company,
what we often confront is
the contradiction between these two.

It is often said in Japan "no one can live on air."
So, as long as we are managing a company,
we must make a profit day by day.
And if not,
we can neither pay employees their salaries nor
continue to exist as a company.

However, on the other hand, it is also said
"Man shall not live by bread alone."
People who happen to come together in a company
devote their lives to this company.
If so,
simply "paying employees their salaries"
is not the sole objective of the company.

To become a company where employees can feel
job satisfaction and joy of working.
It is also an important goal for the company.
And to this end,
it is important to value highly
the social contributions of the company.

However, pursuit of profit and social contribution
often appear as a contradiction
in the management scene.

For example, "price" symbolizes this contradiction.

If a company sells a product at a low price,
the customers will be happy
and it will be able to make a contribution to society.
But, as a result, profits of the company may diminish.
Conversely,
if it takes advantage of the monopolized market,
and sells at a high price, it may gain a large profit.
But sometimes the company will end up being criticized
as an "antisocial business."

However, excellent companies have
an admirable way of coping with such a contradiction.

The "management of contradiction."

The companies practice it in an excellent way.

Then, what kind of management is this?

The "management of contradiction" is management through the "sublation" of contradiction.

No "dichotomic judgment."

That is
the point of the management of contradiction.

This is because if we mechanically
make a dichotomic judgment
to cope with a contradiction,
the life force will be lost.

For example, if we make the dichotomic judgment that
"for a company, pursuit of profit is everything,"
we may realize an increase in
the performance of the company for a short period,
but people will perceive the company as having
no good will and its reputation will be diminished.
And, along with this,
the employees will lose their motivation for working,
and in the long view, both the productivity and
the creativity of the company will be lessened and lost.

However, on the other hand,
if we make the dichotomic judgment that
"for a company, social contribution is everything,"
we will lose sight of our foundation.
Consequently, profits will not go up,
the company cannot continue,
and it will be unable to realize its ideal.

As mentioned above, for the company,
the existence of a "contradiction" is, in a sense,
exactly what generates the "life force" of the company.

Consequently, if a company resolves the contradiction
through a mechanical dichotomic judgment,
it will lose not only the contradiction
but also its life force and its driving force.
Then both progress and development
will stop right there.

And this is a principle that applies to everything,
including the markets and society,
not only to companies.

So, what should we do?
If we do not make such a dichotomic judgment,
what should we do?

We should apply the "sublation" of dialectic.

Then, what does sublation mean?

This is a German term, *"aufheben."*
It refers to a process in which two things, which
appear to mutually contradict and oppose each other,
are elevated to a higher dimension
by affirming, including, integrating and transcending them
without negating one or the other.

Let us discuss this with a concrete example.

The point of the "management of contradiction" is to strike a balance by swinging the pendulum.

Let us take the example of
the contradiction we described earlier,
concerning "pursuit of profit"
and "social contribution" in a company.

To sublate the contradiction between these two means
to not make a dichotomic judgment of
negating one side of either
"pursuit of profit" or "social contribution"
while affirming the other side
but to affirm, include and integrate both of them.
And, by achieving this,
we can create an excellent company.

For example, the following three phrases
that are often spoken in Japanese style management
represent this sublation exactly.

"The company first contributes
to society through its main business."

"Profits are proof of contributing to society."

"The fact that a large profit has been
given to the company
represents a call of the people to use this profit
to make further contributions to society."

These phrases from Japanese style management
deeply represent the management philosophy,
which means to not consider "pursuit of profit"
and "social contributions" as two oppositions,
even if they appear to be mutually contradictory,
but to sublate the contradiction between the two.

Now, if we do not take the viewpoint of
"resolution of contradiction,"
but take the viewpoint of
"sublation of contradiction,"
how should we, as executives and managers
in the actual workplace, pursue correctly
such a management style?
If we should not negate mechanically
one of the two which contradicts the other,
then how should we practice
this management of contradiction?

To put it plainly.

We should swing the "pendulum."

That is, as if a pendulum is swinging
back and forth between two end points,
we should push the pendulum between
the two things which oppose and contradict each other.
In this way, we should strike a balance between them.

When management becomes one sided,
we swing the pendulum in the opposite direction
to bring about an overall balance.

**The "management of contradiction" is needed
not only in corporate management
but also in public administration and politics.**

For example,
contradiction that is often discussed in the company:

"Short-term profits" and "long-term strategies."

The pendulum is needed for this as well.

For example, when the organization as a whole
emphasizes the securing of "short-term profits" so greatly
that they think only of the immediate tasks and
lose sight of the future vision,
executives and managers will venture to insist on
the importance of "long-term strategies."

Conversely, when the organization as a whole
emphasizes the importance of "long-term strategies"
so greatly that they think only of the future vision and
lose sight of the immediate tasks,
executives and managers will rigorously insist on
the importance of "short term profits."

The management of contradiction
that executives and managers need to practice
precisely means to "strike a balance"
between the management tasks viewed as contradictions.
It also means to continue to swing the pendulum
perceiving sensitively the condition of the organization
in order to strike such a balance.

And by continuing to swing the pendulum
and to strike a balance,
executives and managers promote both the
learning of each individual member of the organization
and the learning of the organization as a whole.

Under what conditions or in what situations
should they focus on "short-term profits"
or put emphasis on "long-term strategies?"

Executives and managers must continue
to boldly swing the pendulum
in order that each individual member of the organization
may learn the issues above
to the level of "spontaneous judgment"
and the organization as a whole may learn those issues
to the level of "corporate culture."

And this way of swinging the pendulum
is not sufficient if viewed only from the overall
framework of the company as a whole.
Naturally, whether in the marketing division
or the development division,
the pendulum should be swung for each division
for a different balance.
Sometimes it is necessary to swing the pendulum
for a different balance adjusting to the personality and
the character of each individual employee.

However, in order to practice
this management of contradiction,
executives and managers, in fact, must have
"multiple personality" within themselves.
The meaning of this will be discussed in detail in Chapter 6.

The role of administration is
to strike a balance between
market principles and government regulations.

And this management of contradiction
is not only required of business management.
It is also required of administration and politics.

For example, the contradiction between market principles
and government regulations in government policy.
The management of contradiction of these two is needed for
both politicians and administrators.

That is, the following questions can be raised
concerning services that are to be offered in a society:
To what extent should we entrust to the private sector
and market principles?
To what extent should we expect the government to bear
and treat these services as objects of regulations?

The issue of the optimum balance between
market principles and government regulations
is fundamental for policy making,
and is an issue in state management required of
politicians and administrators.

And in recent years,
in many capitalist countries including Japan,
the introduction of "market principles" and
the realization of "small government" has
become a major political challenge.
At the moment, the pendulum is swinging strongly
in the direction of market principles.

However, if we look at this from a long-term viewpoint,
politicians and administrators must return the swing of
the pendulum at an appropriate point in time
to strike a balance in policy,
by recognizing the conditions of the period.

Consequently, the pendulum is now moving
in the direction of market principles,
naturally, at some appropriate point in the future,
it will need to swing back in
the direction of government regulations.

Another example, the contradiction in politics between
"self responsibility" and "relief for the weak."

In countries such as Japan, which have practiced
a policy of "government regulations" and "big government"
for a long period of time, the people are penetrated with
the consciousness of dependence:
"If I am in trouble, the government would be of help."
But, as large negative influences of such an attitude
come to be pointed out, the pendulum today is swinging
in the direction of "self responsibility" and "self-help."

However, from a long-term viewpoint,
necessarily, at some point,
the pendulum will again swing in the direction of
"relief for the weak" for people who have suffered from
competitions, and people who need aid in an aged society.

But, the most important thing in this management of
contradiction is the judgment of timing:
"At what point in time should the pendulum be swung back?"

We must not forget the importance of this fact.

**With contradiction becoming the life force,
the world
will change, develop and evolve.**

In this way, management of contradiction is
the activity to sublate the contradiction between
two opposing senses of value through continuing to swing
the pendulum between the two,
which means, in the short term,
to strike an overall balance that is optimum
for the current condition, and in the long term,
to realize the growing of the individual,
the learning of the organizations,
and the maturing of society.

This is the basic method of management of contradiction,
which is how to cope with the contradictions
in the society, the markets and the organizations
based on the law of
development through "sublation of contradiction."

And we have already discussed
the idea of dialectic which
lies at the roots of this management of contradiction.

Contradiction is the driving force
for the development of the world.

That is, in order to gain an insight into
the essence of things in this world,
foresee their future, and formulate policies and strategies,
it is important to first look deeply into
the contradictions in front of us that are inherent
in the society, the markets and the organizations.

And it is also important to consider carefully
what will happen from now on in the society,
the markets and the organizations
with this contradiction becoming the driving force.

We should remember.

The world in which we live
is filled with contradictions.

And, contradictions are
the driving forces of the development of the world
and the life forces of the world.
Therefore, the world in which we live
will change, develop, and evolve.

For this reason, we should not mechanically
negate these contradictions.

We must dialectically
sublate these contradictions.

**The capacity of a person
is none other than the "power of the soul"
that can embrace great contradictions.**

Then, in the society, the markets and the organizations,
what is the important wisdom
required of politicians, administrators and executives
in order to cope with these contradictions
and in order to sublate these contradictions?

The noted Buddhist Katsuichiro Kamei
said the following important words:

"Dichotomic judgment is the weakness of the soul."

Certainly, as these words suggest,
we sometimes tend to make dichotomic judgments
when we are confronted with various contradictions, and
find ourselves in distress and confusion.

"First, economic growth is everything."
"There is no help for it, if the weak are selected out."
"Business, after all, is all about making profits."

We tend to escape into such dichotomic judgments.

However, what is essentially required of
such persons as the leaders of society, including
politicians, administrators and executives,
is to continue struggling with
the contradictions in front of them
without escaping from these contradictions.

In other words, what is needed for them in the face of
the various contradictions existing in this society is
to confront them,
to hold them in the core of their minds,
and to continue struggling with them
to find a way to sublate these contradictions
without making dichotomic judgments.

This is exactly the activity for which we need
the caliber to be called the "strength of the soul."

However, when we understand the importance of this,
we will find the true meaning of the words which
from the past have been bestowed upon
outstanding leaders in politics and management.

"A person of great capacity."

This refers to a person who can embrace in his or her mind
great contradictions, confront them,
and continue struggling with them.

This is the kind of person
that these words would be bestowed upon.

**When we acquire "dialectic thinking,"
we also acquire the "ability of dialogue"
to gain an insight into essence through dialogue.**

Now, in order to carry out management of contradiction,
what kind of "ability" is required
for such leaders as
politicians, administrators, and executives?

To put it simply.

It is the "ability of dialectic dialogue."

To put it another way.

Just through dialogue,
our thinking naturally becomes deeper.
And the essence of things becomes apparent.

That is the kind of ability.

And, actually, by understanding "dialectic,"
this ability will be naturally acquired.
Because, as the word "dialectic" itself suggests,
it was born in the age of ancient Greece
as a technique of dialogue.

Who used this "dialectic" was Socrates,
a philosopher well known from *Apology*, written by Plato.

Socrates valued "dialectic" highly
as a technique for searching for the truth.
He used dialectic as a technique
to deepen thinking
and to arrive at the truth through dialogue.

However, this dialectic
is a technique totally different from
"debate" or "discussion."

Debate, literally, is a technique in which people
holding different opinions argue with each other and
attempt to prove one's own argument is correct.

And, discussion is a technique in which people
holding different opinions gather and
learn various viewpoints from each other
through exchanging their opinions.

In contrast to those above, dialectic is a technique
in which people holding opposing opinions
move into deeper thinking through dialogue.
In other words,
this is not a "technique for engaging in an argument,"
but a "technique for deepening thinking."

Then, what is this technique, specifically?

**Thinking becomes deeper
through the process of
"thesis, antithesis, and synthesis."**

This is the deepening of thinking through
"thesis," "antithesis," and "synthesis."

That is, dialectic is
a technique by which people deepen thinking through
the process of "thesis, antithesis, and synthesis."

To put it simply, it is a technique:
Where one person states an opinion (thesis) and
another person states an opposing opinion (antithesis),
and through a dialogue based on each opinion,
both of them arrive at
a deeper understanding (synthesis) including, integrating
and sublating the two opposing opinions.

Let us discuss concretely.

For example, concerning issues in child education,
one person says "in education, kindness is essential."
In response to this, another person says,
"no, in education strictness is essential."

At this stage, their opinions are completely
in opposition and in contradiction with each other.
If the two of them engage in earnest dialogue,
their understanding will deepen further.

For example,
opinions will be offered such as:
"I wonder if not scolding a child means true kindness?"
Or "maybe, occasionally scolding a child strictly could be
real kindness."

Also, on the other hand, opinions will be offered such as:
"In the background of strictness,
there must not be the anger of a scolding person."
Or "in the depths of strictness, there must be a heart
which believes deeply in the potential of the child."

And then, in the midst of exchanging such opinions,
the thinking of both person are deepened,
and the true meaning of the notions of
kindness and strictness
in child education becomes clear.

Ultimately, eyes will be opened to
a deeper level of education which is
neither simply kind,
nor simply strict, but includes, integrates
and sublates these kindness and strictness.

This is "dialectic" as a "technique of dialogue."

"Dialogue"
is a technique of wisdom
which surpasses "debate" and "discussion."

As mentioned above, this dialectic is
neither debate in which we simply engage in
a clash of opinions
nor discussion in which we simply exchange opinions
but an extremely creative technique of dialogue
in the sense that we can deepen each other's thinking.

Consequently,
in our daily "discussion,"
if we apply the technique of "dialectic dialogue,"
our discussions will necessarily become creative ones.

However, the current trends in the world today are
the technique of debate, which is
how to argue down opponents by speaking skills, and
the technique of logical thinking, which is
how to reach a logically correct conclusion.

Of course, these techniques have
their own value and role,
but we must understand the existence of
the "technique of wisdom,"
which is at a higher level
surpassing these techniques.

The technique of "debate" tends to end up being
unproductive, where people cannot humbly learn
from each other and move into deeper thinking,
because debate is, in many cases, limited to situations
where people point out the faults of
the opinions of their opponents and insist on
the superiority of their own opinions over the other.

On the other hand,
since the technique of "logical thinking" basically
emphasizes logical consistency
and eliminates contradictions,
it does not have the viewpoint of sublating contradiction
which is the driving force and the life force of
the development of things.
For this reason, this technique is useful to some degree
in solving simple problems, but is not very useful
as a technique of wisdom for considering
difficult problems in depth and
asking a question that has no answer.

Therefore, if we acquire
the techniques of debate and logical thinking,
we should advance and acquire the techniques of
dialectic dialogue and dialectic thinking.

This is because,
when we acquire this technique of wisdom called dialectic,
for the first time before us will rise
a curtain on a wonderful world of wisdom.

And then, we will be able to
deepen our thinking through dialogue,
gain an insight into the essence of things,
and foresee the future.

Chapter Six

The Future Foreseen by Dialectic Thinking.

12 Paradigm Shifts That Will Happen

In the Future of Human Society.

**When the world achieves "dialectic development,"
a paradigm shift will occur
in the worldview and the value system.**

Up to this point, we have discussed
the "Five Laws" of dialectic.

The law of development through "spiral process."

The law of development through "negation of negation."

The law of development through
"transformation from quantity to quality."

The law of development through
"interpenetration of opposing objects."

The law of development through
"sublation of contradiction."

These are the five laws.

And we have discussed
many different things in this world
ranging from products and services
to markets and economies as well as societies and cultures
change, develop and evolve,
based on these five laws.

Then, if we deeply understand these five laws
and foresee the future by applying the laws,
what kind of future will appear to us?

We shall discuss these issues in this chapter.

However, before this,
we must understand one important thing.
It is "what" we should pay attention to
when we foresee the future.

To state in one word.

It is the "paradigm."

In foreseeing change, development and evolution
in the world,
it is important to
watch from the viewpoint of
what kind of paradigm shift will occur.

This is because both substantial changes and
important changes in the world are always
accompanied by fundamental shift
in the "basic worldview and basic value system,"
namely "paradigm."

Consequently, in this chapter, we will discuss and foresee
by applying these five laws of dialectic,
what kind of paradigm shift will occur
in various fields in the world, and
as a result what kind of future will come.

Let us briefly sketch this future.

The voluntary economy
will merge with the monetary economy
and a "new economic principle" will emerge.

What we should first foresee is
the paradigm shift in economies.

What will happen in the field of economies from now?

We have already discussed this in Chapter 1.

The "voluntary economy" will revive.

That is,
the "voluntary economy," which is an economic activity
created by people seeking the "satisfaction of mind"
based on goodwill and affection,
will revive as a mainstream economic activity in society
and increase its influence.

And it will increase its influence on society relative to
the "monetary economy," which is an economic activity
created by people seeking the "acquisition of money"
and has been the mainstream in capitalist societies
up to now.

Now, why will this happen?

We can foresee this from
the law of development through "spiral process."

Namely, the "gift economy" that was
the oldest economic principle for humankind.
This old nostalgic economic principle will revive,
based on the law of spiral development,
accompanied by "new values."

Then, what will happen after this "revival?"

The "voluntary economy" and the "monetary economy"
will merge together.

And then, a "new economic principle" will emerge.

This can also be easily foreseen by a dialectic law,
the law of development through
"interpenetration of opposing objects."

That is, "things which oppose and compete with each other
come to resemble each other."
As stated by this law,
these two economic principles will interpenetrate,
and will merge into one economic principle.

And, in fact, it is no longer what is only foreseen.
It has already become a real trend.

Why is this?

Because the "Web 2.0 revolution" has occurred.

The Web 2.0 revolution
as the new stage in the "Net revolution."
This information revolution sweeping the globe now
has already produced many concrete cases
for this new economic principle.

"Business models"
will evolve into
"social systems."

For example, the Amazon bookseller site.

The business model of this site has already
brought about very high profits.
It is an excellent business model
representing the monetary economy.

Then, on this site,
what kind of service is enjoying
the greatest popularity among users?

The "book review service."

This is a very useful service for users
who are planning to purchase books,
and this has greatly increased
the value of the Amazon site.

However, these "reviews" actually were
not written by Amazon.
These reviews are "grassroots reviews" that are
written spontaneously and without compensation
by the people using this site themselves.

In fact, this is produced by the voluntary economy.

The Amazon business model is, in fact,
what should be called a "social system" based on
a totally new economic principle that is a merging of
the monetary economy and the voluntary economy.

And this merging has not only occurred in Amazon.
The grassroots movie sites, such as YouTube,
the grassroots photo sites, such as Flickr,
all of these business models that use
so-called "UGC" (User Generated Contents)
are social systems based on
this "new economic principle."
And, in this sense, Google, which is
the largest Net business at the present time, is
essentially a business model that uses UGC which was
made public through worldwide sites and blogs.
It is, after all, a social system based on
this "new economic principle."

Now, what about Linux which is regarded as
a representative of the voluntary economy?
This also actually achieved the merging with
the monetary economy.
The reason is as follows:
Linux itself is a software that has been developed by
many computer engineers gathering voluntarily from
all over the world and contributing their efforts
without compensation, but through offering various
services to companies that introduce Linux,
business models of many IT companies have been created.

Then, is the merging of these two economies a movement
only in the world of the Web 2.0 revolution?

Not at all.

**The trends of CSR and social entrepreneurship
symbolize the merging of
the voluntary economy and the monetary economy.**

Now, if we take a broad view of society,
great trends have developed in the direction of
the merging of these two,
both from the monetary economy side
and from the voluntary economy side.
These are the two trends that we discussed in Chapter 1.

One is a trend of
"corporate social responsibility" (CSR).

This is a trend which demands
"social responsibility" of for-profit businesses,
and moreover, requires
"social contribution" in the activities of companies.
It has become a worldwide trend represented by
the activity of ISO establishing
international standards for CSR.

And in the midst of this worldwide trend of CSR,
many companies are developing activities for social
contributions using part of their profits, and are
implementing policies to encourage
their employees as well to join volunteer activities.

This is, in a sense, a trend that
the monetary economy is incorporating
the voluntary economy into itself.

Another is a trend of "social entrepreneurship."

This also has become a worldwide trend,
which has emerged to solve the problems
that conventional non-profit organizations,
foundations and volunteer organizations were faced with.

Conventionally, such non-profit organizations
have operated proclaiming "social contributions."
But since they have operated relying on
benefactors contribution and government supports,
they have been faced with the problem that
they could not continue their activities
if those contributions and supports were cut off.
And then, what has been born reflecting on these problems
is "social entrepreneurship," which adopts
the management technique of entrepreneurship
in the operation of their organizations, creates profits from
their own operations of social contribution, and thus
aims at securing the independence and sustainability of
their activities.

That is, social entrepreneurship is, in a sense,
a trend that the voluntary economy is incorporating
the monetary economy into itself.

The case of the Web 2.0 revolution.
The case of CSR.
The case of social entrepreneurship.
As symbolized by these examples,
in various fields of society today,
a new economic principle has been born
through the merging of the monetary economy and
the voluntary economy,
and now it is penetrating all corners of society.

**In order to solve the global warming problem,
the creation and application of
a "new economic principle" are required.**

In fact, it is of an extremely great significance that
this "new economic principle" is born in this age.

Because this new economic principle is
a highly useful solution for
the global environmental problems, including
the global warming, which confront the world now.

As a main economic method to solve these problems,
the method called "internalization of external economies"
has been adopted until now.

To explain concretely, this method is as follows:

In modern society, various costs
including damage to health, social uneasiness,
environmental measures and environmental remediation,
are generated by environmental pollution and destruction.
They are called "social costs" or "external diseconomies,"
and originally exist "external" of the market economy.

To these external diseconomies,
by introducing an environmental regulation
based on the "polluter-pays principle,"
government demands of companies responsible for
environmental pollution to bear the costs of
environmental measures, environmental remediation and
compensation for health damage,
and reflect them in the cost of their products and services.

By these methods, social costs and external diseconomies
were incorporated into the market economy,
and environmental measures were promoted
through the market principle.
This method is called
"internalization of external economies."

To state in another way, it is a method by which
the social costs and external diseconomies existing
outside of the monetary economy
were incorporated into the monetary economy.

Of course, this is one extremely effective method, and
has been employed in solving the global warming problem
such as "emissions trading."
But actually, in the coming age, one other
economic method will become more important.

This is a method of applying a "new economic principle"
that is the merging of
the monetary economy and the voluntary economy.

In other words, it is a method for aiming at solving
the global environmental problems
not by "internalizing" the volunteer economy existing
outside of the monetary economy
but by "merging" these two economic principles.

To put it concretely, it is a technique for promoting
the solution of the global warming problem
by connecting business models of the private company
with the volunteer minds of grassroots consumers.

Then, what kind of technique is this?

"Corporate currency" and "local currency" are accelerating a new economic principle.

One example of this is a "carbon offset product,"
which is spreading rapidly around the world.

This kind of product is as follows:
A company promises to use a part of the selling price of
the product to reduce the identical amount of CO_2
that is emitted during the manufacturing of that product.

As concrete measures, various methods have been
suggested such as forestation, forest conservation,
investment in natural energy, direct capture of CO_2,
emission trading, and so forth.
These products are, in a sense, aimed at connecting
the "market needs" of the consumer which is the
"people's wish to purchase products they want" with
the "voluntary mind" of the consumer which is the
"people's wish to conserve the global environment."
In other words, it is a new social system which is
created by the merging of the monetary economy
and the voluntary economy.

And, in the midst of this trend,
companies have appeared that use "corporate currency"
for the global warming countermeasures
and the global environment conservation.
Corporate currency means service points that
companies give to the purchasers of their products.

This is a system in which consumers can ask a company
to use corporate currency
for conservation of the global environment,
instead of using it for their own sake.

Furthermore, this trend has brought about a new system
in which consumers can contribute their own
"corporate currency" to social entrepreneurs,
NPOs and NGOs.
This trend will join together with a worldwide trend of CSR
and promote the evolution of corporate currency greatly
from now.

And another example is "local currency."
This is, like corporate currency, a system that is
spreading in various localities around the world
to promote the voluntary economy in each locality.
These trends of local currency and corporate currency
will also connect with each other and merge together
in order to promote the activation of
the voluntary economy.

Then, what will such trends of corporate currency and
local currency bring about from now?

An evolution in the "consciousness" of people
towards "currency."

That is, up to now, for many people in the world
"currency" was merely
a "means to satisfy their own desires."
However, from now on, many people will begin to
understand that "currency" is a "means to change society."
So they will change their consciousness towards currency
and move toward specific actions.

Innovation itself will evolve
from "beneficiary innovation"
to "participatory innovation."

Now, what is the next paradigm shift
that will occur in these trends?

A paradigm shift in "innovation."

That is, from now on,
"spiral development" and "regression to the origin"
will occur also in innovation.

Then, what kind of regression to the origin will occur?

Many people will come to participate
in the process of innovation in society.

Such regression to the origin will occur.

In past times, in communities of older societies,
the wisdom for improving the communities was
discussed freely and equally
among their members.

However, as modern times come along,
"specialization" has occurred.

That is, as specialist knowledge
for solving problems became sophisticated and
that specialist knowledge became
the exclusive domain of only a limited number of people,
naturally, "specialists" in various fields came into being.
And the wisdom of these small number of people
came to create innovations for changing
the community and the society in their respective fields.

However, in the coming age, many people
will come to participate in the innovation process again.

Then, why will such regression to the origin occur?

This is also because
the "Web 2.0 revolution" has occurred.

In other words,
because through this revolution,
people have come to be able to get most of the knowledge,
which is necessary for solving their problems
in communities and societies, on the Web.
And because, through the Web,
many people have come to be able to
offer their own knowledge and wisdom as well as
opinions and ideas to communities and societies.

That is, many people have come to be able to participate
in the innovation process in communities and societies.

The words which symbolize this
are expressed in the world of
the "Web 2.0 revolution."

Through the "Web 2.0 revolution" the age of "collective intelligence" and "wisdom of crowds" will begin.

"Open source."
"Community solution."
"Prosumer-based development."

These are the words.

"Open source" refers to a method
to find solutions of problems through raising questions
widely to society as a whole
and gathering knowledge and wisdom not only from
professional engineers in companies or
policy specialists in government
but also from the general public at large, for example,
in the development of software such as Linux and
the planning of government policy,

Similarly, "community solution" refers to a method
to arrive at solutions through raising questions
in communities in which many people gather
and through getting the members of the communities
to solve their problems
by exchanging their opinions and ideas
freely and voluntarily.

"Prosumer-based development" refers to a method,
which was advocated prophetically in 1980
by the futurologist Alvin Toffler
in his work *The Third Wave,*
to develop new products through collaboration between
the producer and the consumer.

In this way, in the world of the "Web 2.0 revolution,"
a great paradigm shift is occurring now.

From "beneficiary innovation"
to "participatory innovation."

That is the paradigm shift.

Now, the paradigm shift is occurring
from "beneficiary innovation" in which
a small number of specialists and researchers
create innovations while a large number of people
merely receive benefits from those innovations
to "participatory innovation" in which
a large number of people participate
in the process of innovation through offering
their own knowledge and wisdom.

That is,
the method of innovation itself
is in the process of innovation now.
And the words symbolizing this innovation
in the "Web 2.0 revolution" are as follows:

"Wisdom of crowds."
"Collective intelligence."

A paradigm shift will occur
from "indirect democracy"
to "direct democracy."

That is, in the coming age,
not only the knowledge of a small number of specialists
but also the knowledge and wisdom of
a large number of people at the grassroots
will become the driving forces
to solve the problems in society and change society.

Those two words mean that.

And, this is the essence of
the paradigm shift from "beneficiary innovation"
to "participatory innovation"
brought about by the Web 2.0 revolution.

However, if we understand the essence of
this paradigm shift in innovation,
we should also understand that it will naturally
bring about another paradigm shift.

A paradigm shift in "democracy."

Then, what does the paradigm shift
in democracy mean?

From "indirect democracy"
to "direct democracy."

This paradigm shift will occur.

But, when described in this way,
many readers will most likely think as follows:

> In the field of politics,
> indirect democracy by the "representative system"
> will come to an end and direct democracy will begin,
> in which many people will participate in politics
> by using the Web.

Certainly, such a trend will occur.
It is a trend called "digital democracy."

However, what we should discuss here is
not democracy in the field of "politics."

We unconsciously think of the term "democracy"
as a political term.
But that is by no means the case.

That is because, in the coming age,
both in the world of "economy"
and in the world of "culture,"
"democracy" will be realized, furthermore,
"direct democracy" will be realized.

Why is this?

**Direct democracy will spread
not only in the field of politics,
but also in the fields of economy and culture.**

The reason for this
is the participatory innovation mentioned above.

Through the realization of this
participatory innovation,
direct democracy will be finally realized
both in the field of economy and in the field of culture.

Conversely, until now
both in the field of economy and in the field of culture
various activities have been operated
through indirect democracy by the representative system.

For example, for a particular product,
even though
the needs of the consumers were of great variety,
a company would study the customer needs
through market surveys, narrow down the specification
and design of the product, and produce it.
Consequently, consumers were forced to purchase
a "product that most closely met their own needs"
from a limited variety of products.

However, through the "Web 2.0 revolution,"
this situation has changed greatly.

The reason is as follows:
Through this revolution,
"prosumer-based development" will spread,
"Long Tail marketing" will become popular,
and "high mix, low volume production"
will be implemented.
So, in the coming age, consumers will be able to
design, order, and purchase products that they want
as "products made just for themselves."

This means that
direct democracy in economy will be realized.
What will be realized from now is
not conventional "representative, indirect democracy,"
in which a company bringing out products most close
to consumer needs would gain support of consumers,
but "participatory, direct democracy,"
in which consumers directly express their needs and
purchase products realizing their needs.

And, the same paradigm shift will occur
in the field of culture.

For example, in the great trend of the culture of "music,"
the system has been adopted in which a major music label
or music production would discover star musicians,
cultivate them,
promote them by massive advertisement
and create a great boom in the market.

However, this system will also be changed greatly
through the Web 2.0 revolution.

**Democracy will deepen
from the participation of people in "decision-making"
to the participation of people in "social change."**

This change will be caused by following two movements:

Firstly, unknown musicians have become able to
individually and freely produce their original songs,
perform them and make them public through websites
without asking the help of major music labels and
music productions.

Secondly, if their songs are so good as to arouse
the empathy of the public, in the world of the Web,
the evaluation and reputation of them will spread rapidly
among many people and the musicians will be able to
create a new culture in the world of music.

This is a trend which will be born commonly
in the world of creation and art
not only in the world of music
but also in the world of painting and photography,
computer graphics and movies,
as well as in the world of novels and poetry.

In other words, this means that
through the Web 2.0 revolution,
an age has begun in which
even grassroots people
can freely engage in the activity of creation and art
to express themselves
and freely make public their works to society.

And if creation and art can be cultivated
both by the people who create and produce them
and by the people who appreciate and criticize them,
then, the "Web 2.0 revolution"
has opened the curtain on an age
in which grassroots people can participate in both sides.

To state in another way,
direct democracy will be realized
not only in the world of politics and economy,
but also in the world of creation of culture.

However, this never means
that professional creators and artists,
superior viewers and critics will become unnecessary.

Just like the fact that
a high mountain always has a broad foot below it,
the more people will participate in
such worlds of creation of culture,
the higher the standards of the professional
will become in the world.

In this way, if we understand
that direct democracy will be realized from now on
not only in the world of politics
but also in the worlds of economy and culture,
then we will have to understand the most important ideas
in the depths of the word of "democracy."

Democracy does not simply mean that
many people participate in "decision-making."
Democracy does mean that
many people participate in "social change."

The curtain will rise on
the age of "non-linguistic communication" and
"image communication."

Let us discuss next a paradigm shift in "communication."

Now, what will happen in the field of communication
from now?

In this field as well, "spiral development" will occur.
As a result,
"nostalgic communication" will revive.

What kind of communication will this be?

"Non-linguistic communication."

That is, in the coming age,
communication that does not use "language" will spread.

This is obvious by looking at the world of
the "Web 2.0 revolution."

For example, YouTube, which is accessed by
an overwhelming number of people around the world.
On this site, an infinite number of grassroots movies are
uploaded, most of which are not messages expressed
in texts or words but messages expressed in movies.

Similarly, the grassroots photo site Flickr
enjoying high popularity now, is the site
in which most of the uploaded contents are not
messages expressed in texts or words but
non-linguistic messages expressed in photos.

Also, even in websites and blogs,
both delivering messages and expressing oneself
through photos, movies, music, and sound
are increasing rapidly.

What is happening here?

The age of "image communication."

It is about to begin.

A culture in which
people convey their messages not through texts and words
but through photos, movies, music and sound.
That is, a culture in which people convey
their messages through non-linguistic information
and image information is about to spread.

And this is, in a sense, a regression to the origin of
the culture of humankind prior to the creation of language.
However, remember,
this is "spiral development" as well.
It is obviously a regression to the origin that has
"climbed up one step higher."
An advanced culture of non-linguistic communication
will be born, in which
modern sophisticated media technology is used.

Then, as a result, what will happen?

A paradigm shift will occur
from ability for "thinking" and "logic"
to ability for "feeling" and "intuition."

From the "culture of thinking"
to the "culture of feeling."

Such a paradigm shift will occur.
And as a result of this paradigm shift,

Not only the ability
to think about something "logically"
by reading texts and words,
but also the ability
to feel something "intuitively"
by viewing photos and movies
will be refined.

However, we must not misunderstand this.
This never means that our "ability for language"
or "ability for logical thinking" will diminish.

What will happen from now is definitely
"dialectic development."

Different abilities which appear to be "in opposition"
will become "integrated" and "sublated."

That is,

"Ability for thinking" versus "ability for feeling."
"Ability for logic" versus "ability for intuition."
"Reason" versus "sensibility."

Such abilities considered previously as two opposites
will become integrated in us as one single ability.

If we think back, in the industrial society or
knowledge society until now,
it has been emphasized
in school and corporate education
to develop our own abilities for
"thinking," "logic" and "reason."

However, in the post-knowledge society from now,
it will become more important to develop the abilities for
"feeling," "intuition" and "sensibility" rather than
the abilities mentioned above.
In this sense, in the trend of "image communication"
created by the "Web 2.0 revolution,"
we will realize an ideal balance in terms of
developing our abilities as human beings.

In recent years, these words have been often discussed:

"Left brain" versus "right brain."

These words need to be considered carefully
from the viewpoint of dialectic sublation.

The "da Vinci society" will arrive, where anyone can develop various talents in the manner of Leonardo da Vinci.

Now, what will happen in our lives from now on?

From the monetary economy to the voluntary economy.
From beneficiary innovation to participatory innovation.
From indirect democracy to direct democracy.
From linguistic communication
to non-linguistic communication.
From the culture of thinking to the culture of feeling.

When such paradigm shifts occur,
just what kinds of changes will happen
in each of our lives?

From "single talent"
to "multiple talent."

The paradigm shift will occur.
That is, instead of leading a life which develops
"only a single talent,"
we will be able to lead a life which can develop
"various talents."

This is because, through the various kinds of
paradigm shifts discussed above,
we can, for example, lead such kinds of lives as follows:

In the daytime, we work as managers in a company,
on the weekends, we work as members of NPOs or NGOs.
And, when we have time, as individual consumers,
we belong to the Web communities which carry out
prosumer-based development and we join in developing
new products interacting with the companies.
Moreover, in our own blogs, we deliver various messages
and enjoy comments from many people.
Also, we make public our own photos on websites,
and occasionally we perform our own songs
and release them in our own blogs.

We will be able to lead such lives.
If so, what kind of society will arrive from now?
We could venture to say,

The "da Vinci society."

Leonardo da Vinci, the multitalented genius
who was the outstanding figure in the Italian Renaissance.

This is a society
in which we can develop the various talents
sleeping inside us, express ourselves freely,
and make public our works to society
in various fields including hobbies and learning,
science and technology, art and music, prose and poetry,
even if each of us is not a genius like da Vinci.
Moreover, everyone will be able to participate in
the creation of the culture of their society.
Such a society will arrive from now on.

**The "post persona society" will arrive,
where anyone
can live various personalities.**

Then, in such a "da Vinci society,"
what will happen next?

From a "single personality,"
to a "multiple personality."

This paradigm shift will occur.

This is because, in essence, for human beings,
"talent" and "personality" are two sides of the same coin.

In other words,
developing the "talent"
needed for one profession or job is,
at the same time,
developing the "personality"
needed for that profession or job.

For example, working as a manager,
a "leadership personality" in that person is developed.
Working as an social entrepreneur,
an "empathic personality" in that person is developed.
Working as a musician,
a "sensory personality" in that person is developed.

Therefore, in the "da Vinci society,"
we will cultivate various "talents," and at the same time
we will also cultivate various "personalities"
sleeping inside us.

And actually,
these will bring about a great paradigm shift in our lives.

Because, in society up to now,
in many cases, we were living a single personality.
In order to make our life and work go smoothly,
we would often choose the most suitable "persona,"
and by wearing it, we would try to avoid
conflict with others and confusion in our lives.

However, as a result, what has happened?

"Suppression."

We have noticed the existence of many "personalities"
within our self through various experiences in our lives.
But since living these personalities
in real daily work and life very often actually
causes misunderstandings and confusion,
we have been living while suppressing most of them and
avoiding exposure of them.

> **To discover, accept and express**
> **the "hidden self"**
> **is none other than "catharsis."**

However, that situation changed
through the Web 2.0 revolution.

Because, through this revolution,
we have become able to live various personalities
without creating confusion in our daily work and life,
and without producing misunderstandings
from those around us.

In the daytime,
we live a personality as a manager in a company,
on the weekends,
we live a personality as a social entrepreneur.
In the world of the Web, we lead our life as a designer
participating in product development,
and on our own blogs, we lead our life
as a novelist or essayist.
And at times we lead our life as a photographer
holding an exhibition on websites
or as a musician performing our own songs on websites.

In this way,
we can live and express the various personalities
which we suppressed behind our "persona" until now.
Such a "post persona society" will arrive.

Then, why does this have important meaning?

Because it is "catharsis."

To discover the "suppressed self" or the "hidden self,"
accept it, and express it.

Because, this is a profound catharsis for a person.

Despite this, in society up to now,
most people have been required to
live a "single personality."

It was, in a sense, needed to maintain social order,
while it caused unconscious "suppression"
deep in the minds of people.
And at times, it caused individual mental illness,
at other times, it manifested itself
as a social-psychological illness.

Of course, we should not forget that
the Web 2.0 revolution will not solve all the problems of
individual illness and social illness
and that social-psychological illnesses unique to
the world of the Web can arise.
But the revolution has made us notice
that there exists
a complex system inside of our minds.

It is an "ecosystem of mind."

That is, various personalities exist in our minds
and they form a single "ecosystem."

Then, what does this mean?

**Management of the ecosystem of mind
will allow the abilities of
human beings to flower.**

The coexistence of "diverse values."

This is the meaning.

That is, it means to accept the coexistence of
"diverse values" within ourselves that we discover,
accept and express the "diverse personalities"
within ourselves.

And this has one important meaning.

Because, when we embrace the diverse personalities
and accept the coexistence of
diverse values within ourselves,
a wonderful thing will happen.

The "flowering of abilities."

Because that will happen.

For example, abilities of imagination and creativity,
insight and intuition, sensibility and empathy,
expression and communication.
These abilities will flower within us.

For example, outstanding creators in art and literature,
excellent leaders in management and politics, and
superior innovators in science and engineering.
All of them create wonderful works through
embracing "multiple selves" inside of them and
through contradiction and conflict,
dialogue and collaboration, among their multiple selves.

However,
to embrace the diverse personalities inside oneself and
to accept the coexistence of diverse values
is not so easy a process as we state it.
This is exactly
an experience of very painful psychological process of
struggling with contradictions and
conflict between opposing values,
as most of these people have experienced.

And for that very reason, this psychological process,
in many cases, will be tied to
the growth and maturation as a person.

Consequently, in the coming age,
how to discover, accept, and express
the various personalities in ourselves,
how to manage the ecosystem of mind that
consists of those various personalities,
these will become important concerns in our lives.

And these actually
will become very important concerns
not only for individuals
but also for the whole society.

Why is this?

**The coexistence of diverse values in the individual mind
will realize
the coexistence of diverse values in the whole society.**

This is because the "coexistence of diverse values" will
be required of the whole society as well.

Especially today, in advanced nations that
proclaim democracy,
many people believe that
cultivating a lot of diverse values and accepting them
in their society
is a proof of the maturity of their society.

This stems from a deep reflection on the fact that
in the history of the 20th century,
nations that were tainted with a single ideology
oppressed people who did not accept it,
invaded other nations that did not agree with it,
and caused calamitous wars.

However, if we watch
the realities of the world in the 21st century,
even nations that advocate the importance of
"diverse values," in fact, have been spreading
specific form of capitalist principles around the world,
under the slogan of "globalization."

And, with the end of the Cold War,
the old ideological opposition between
"capitalism" and "communism" came to an end,
but as we see in the world conditions since 9.11,
a new form of ideological opposition has begun between
"Christianity" and "Islam."

Then, why have "deviations towards a single set of values"
ironically occurred in societies
where the "coexistence of diverse values" is advocated?

The reason is actually obvious.

Because, in the minds of each of us,
such a "coexistence of diverse values"
has not yet been realized.

In society as a whole, no matter how much it is said
that the coexistence of diverse values is important,
if each individual cannot accept diverse values
in his or her mind,
secret prejudices and contempt
as well as enmity and conflict will continue
in obscure corners of society.
And when a single value system acquires power,
a tendency will often arise to force the value system on
society as a whole.

For this reason, in the coming age,
the management of the ecosystem of mind in individuals
will become vital.

A paradigm shift will occur
from "ideology"
to "cosmology."

Then, through this,
what kind of paradigm shift will occur
in society?

From "ideology"
to "cosmology."

That is the paradigm shift.

That is, what we learned from the failures of
the great social experiments of the 20th century is that
the paradigm, in which the "ideologies" being proud of
their steadfast value systems
clashed and fought with each other
and attempted to
assimilate the world into a single ideology,
exposed its limitations and came to an end.

Then, what kind of paradigm should spread
throughout the world in the 21st century
in place of this "ideology paradigm?"

It is the "cosmology paradigm."

That is, not to reject any of the various value systems
existing in the world, but to accept all of them.

It is the paradigm that
learns the respective good points of the
various value systems and incorporates them,
and appreciates the new values that will emerge through
the encounters of the various value systems.

In recent years, the importance of "pluralism"
that accepts the diversity of value systems is mentioned
by many intellects.
But, often, the words "coexistence of diverse values"
have been misunderstood and used in the sense of
"tolerating different values
and accepting their coexistence."

However, the true meaning of these words is
"recognizing the coexistence of different values
as the greatest value"
and this is none other than the cosmology paradigm.

In Chapter 1
we discussed that
"the essence of evolution is diversification."

Now, in the same sense,
the evolution of the society in which we live means
the diversification of the value systems in our societies.
And by this diversification,
the evolution of society will be accelerated,
the future possibilities for evolution will expand,
and a truly "wealthy society" will be realized.

Then, when this paradigm shift
from ideology to cosmology occurs,
what kind of paradigm shift will occur
in the world of "religion?"

Monotheistic religious systems
will regress to their origin,
to polytheistic religious systems.

From "monotheism"
to "polytheism."

This paradigm shift will occur.

Why will this occur?

Because the laws of dialectic also apply,
without exception, to the development of religion as well.

That is, the law of spiral development.

It will happen.

In other words,
old religions will revive in new forms.

That is polytheism.

To discuss polytheism,
we need to ask one basic question.
What kind of religion was the earliest one
if we look back in the history of humankind?

It was "animism,"
which considered that gods and spirits
resided in everything in the world.

And what appeared after "animism"
was "polytheism" in which various gods existed
as symbolized in Greek and Roman mythology.

But that polytheism, in the course of world history,
relinquished its primary status to
the monotheisms such as
Judaism, Christianity, and Islam.

A major reason for this was that the doctrine of
monotheism was established
on the basis of a clear single value system,
and came to have a consistent refined system
for leading many people into the world of faith.

However, in all things,
a strong point is always a weak point as well.

Monotheistic religion,
since it is a system with a clear value system
and a consistent doctrine,
always created the problem that
it could not coexist with other monotheistic religions.

This was the reason
for the disputes between religions
and wars between religious states
that have been repeated throughout world history.

Religious systems
will evolve into a religious system at a metalevel,
based on the principle of "cosmology."

Then, what will happen to this monotheism?

A "spiral development" will occur.

From "polytheism" to "monotheism,"
and again,
from "monotheism" to "polytheism."

This regression to the origin will occur.

Remember again,
this is also dialectic development,
spiral development.

A revival of polytheism in a new dimension.
And dialectic sublation of monotheism and polytheism.

That will happen.

If so,
what form will it take?

The various monotheisms existing in the world
will not negate other doctrines,
will accept the existences of other doctrines,
will understand the basic commonalities of
various doctrines
and will coexist in the world.

In this way, a polytheism in a new dimension
will emerge in the world.

Aldus Huxley once showed the insight that
many religions which had emerged in
human history speak common truths
in the foundations of their doctrines,
in his *The Perennial Philosophy*.

The "polytheism" that will revive from now
will become a religious system at a metalevel,
which understands the common truths
in various monotheistic doctrines,
does not negate any doctrine
and accepts every doctrine.

And this new religious system will
go beyond the two opposites of
"monotheism" and "polytheism"
and become an evolved religious system
through sublating these two dialectically.

In a sense, this will become the trend
to occur at the same time as
the paradigm shift from ideology to cosmology
mentioned earlier.

The Gaia thought, a major concern of this period of the global environmental problems, is a revival of the ancient "animism" in a new form.

However, when considering the evolution of
religious systems in the 21st century,
we need to understand one more interesting trend:

The spiral development of "animism."

As mentioned earlier,
the animism,
in which gods and spirits reside in everything,
was regarded as "worship by uncivilized people" or
"primitive religion" and faded away
in the course of the appearance of polytheism and
the evolution of religious systems into monotheism.

But this "animism"
revived from the unexpected world
late in the 20th century.

From the world of "science."

It revived in the scientific world
in the setting of major issues that humankind faces now:
The global environmental problems.

Then, in what form did it revive?

The Gaia thought.

That is, the scientific theory stating
"the Earth itself is a gigantic living system"
was advocated by the British scientist, James Lovelock,
and has gained the support of many scientists.

Lovelock has accumulated research results for many years,
and proposed that the system called the Earth
is a gigantic "living system" that has homeostasis.

In other words, it is the idea that life resides in
everything in this world, this Earth.
This is, in a sense, spiral development of
the nostalgic animism and a revival of it
in a more sophisticated form.

And when we examine the revival of animism
and the regression to polytheism,
we will notice another interesting fact.

It is a worldview that has been stated in
Buddhist thought for thousands of years.

The words
"in mountains, rivers, grass, trees, lands: everywhere
resides the Buddha nature, no matter where."

This is the idea that "the Buddha nature" resides in
everything on the Earth, as does "life" itself.
This is, in a sense,
"sophisticated animism."

And this Buddhist thought is also a religious system that
already has involved "Mahayana thought" in its basis,
which is the cosmological principle
that incorporates all doctrines and ideas within itself.

A paradigm shift will occur
from the "mechanical system worldview"
to the "living system worldview."

In this way,
when "religion" undergoes a paradigm shift,
what kind of paradigm shift will "science" itself undergo?

This has already been discussed since the 1960s.

From the "mechanical system worldview"
to the "living system worldview."

That is, it is a paradigm shift from the worldview
regarding this world as a "gigantic machine"
to the worldview regarding the world
as a "great living system."

The reason this paradigm shift
has come to be needed in science is
that "reductionism," which has been the basis of science
until now, faces its limits.

"Reductionism" is based on the belief that
we could understand the nature of the world
if we decompose this world, like a machine, into
small components, analyze each component carefully
and finally synthesize the results.

But this research method faces its limits.

In other words,
this world is like an organic living system,
and by the procedure of decomposing and analyzing it,
its original nature is lost.
As a result, it becomes impossible
to understand its nature.
This problem was pointed out as the limit of
"reductionism."

This is a problem which is symbolized by the fact that
we cannot understand the causes of psychosomatic illnesses
just by detailed physical examination nor can
we understand group psychological phenomena
just by the psychoanalysis of individuals.

Consequently, the limit of this reductionism
was proclaimed from as early as the 1960s
as a basic criticism of science.
Also it was proclaimed in different forms
as a criticism of the Newtonian paradigm
based on Newtonian mechanics, and of
the Descartes paradigm
presupposing the separation of mind and body.

On the other hand, though "holism," which was proposed
as a criticism of such reductionism,
was agreeable as one idea,
it lacked any specific methodology to implement it.

However, in the 1980s, the specific methodology,
interestingly enough, was born from the midst of
the modern science itself that holism was criticizing.

The science of complex systems will bring about
the evolution of modern science into
the science of the "living system paradigm."

What is that?

The science of "complex systems."

This is a leading edge science and
an extremely broad interdisciplinary research
begun at the Santa Fe Institute
established in New Mexico, the US, in 1984
by three Nobel Prize winners,
Murray Gell-man, Philip Anderson and Kenneth Arrow.

Then, what are complex systems?

There are words which teach us its meaning:

"When things become complex,
they acquire new properties."

Just as the words suggest,
including all of nature, society, and humans,
when such systems become complex,
they acquire "new properties,"
which are not the "simple sum" of
the properties of their constituent components.

And, to research these "new properties" that
complex systems acquire is one of the objectives of
the science of complex systems.

Then, what are these "new properties?"

The cultural anthropologist, Gregory Bateson,
showed the profound insight:

"In complex things, life dwells."

As these words suggest, when all systems,
including nature, society, and humans, become complex,
they begin to manifest as "living systems"
with properties of self organization, emergence, coherence,
evolution, co-evolution, and the formation of ecosystems.

And, to elucidate this phenomenon is
the ultimate objective of complex systems science.

Now what will happen through the emergence and
development of "complex systems science?"

This is the paradigm shift in "science,"
as discussed earlier.

From the "mechanical system worldview"
to the "living system worldview."

However,
this paradigm shift to the living system worldview is,
in fact, about to occur
not only at the leading edge of "science"
but also at the leading edge of "technology."

The Internet revolution will promote
the evolution of organizations, markets and societies
into sophisticated complex systems.

So, what is the leading edge of "technology?"

The Internet revolution.

Then, why will this revolution promote the paradigm shift
to the living system worldview?

Because the Internet will transform all
"social systems" into "living systems."

That is, because the Internet will enhance
the interrelationships among the internal constituents
in the systems of organizations, markets and societies,
enhance the complexity of these systems,
and promote their properties as "complex systems."
Consequently, the Internet will promote the properties of
self organization, emergence, coherence, evolution,
co-evolution and the formation of ecosystems
in those systems.

For example, in the Internet world,
the following phenomena will occur everywhere:

"Self organization of the Net communities."
"Emergence of new knowledge in communities."
"Coherent behavior of many people through the Internet."
"Co-evolution of the culture of the company and
the consciousness of the consumer."
"Formation of product ecosystems at portal sites."

Then, as a result, what will happen?

The permeation of the "living system worldview" into
the consciousness of people.

This will happen.

That is, as people engage in the activities
in the Internet world,
the consciousness of people will naturally transform
into the "living system worldview."

If so, what will be needed as a result?

The wisdom to cope with the living system.

This will be needed.

For example, in living systems such as organizations,
markets and societies,
wisdom to promote self organization of communities,
wisdom to promote emergence of new knowledge,
wisdom to generate coherence among people,
wisdom to promote the formation of ecosystems,
such wisdom will come to be needed.

The wisdom to cope with the living system
will be needed
to solve the global environmental problems.

However, in the coming age,
in addition to the Internet revolution,
there is another important reason that
the wisdom to cope with the living system will be needed.

The global environmental problems, including
the "global warming."

This problem will also require us to learn
the wisdom to cope with the living system.

There are two reasons for this.

The first reason is that the Earth itself is
the "largest living system."

That is,
as described by James Lovelock in his Gaia thought,
the Earth itself is
a gigantic living system with homeostasis and is
the most sophisticated complex system that
nature has created over 4.6 billion years.

Therefore, if we want to engage in
solving the global environmental problems,
first of all, we will need to learn the wisdom
to cope with the "gigantic living system."

The second reason is that
the global environmental problems themselves form
an "extremely highly complex system."

That is, the global environmental problems are
highly complex issues, involving a very large number of
elements including the Earth, nature, society, culture,
economies, politics, institutions, organizations,
technology and science.
To solve them, we need the wisdom to cope with
"highly complex systems," that is,
the wisdom to cope with the "sophisticated living system."

Taking "change in human lifestyle"
as just one example often stated as a solution to
the global environmental problems,
what is necessary to make such change in lifestyle will
not be pressure by government from above, but will be
movement created from among the people themselves
in spontaneously, self-organizing and emergent ways.

But, for this, we will need to adopt
a "policy of emergence" or a "strategy of emergence"
combining various types of approaches as follows:

Development and provision of inexpensive and easy-to-use
environmental technologies,
introduction of economic incentive systems
to promote change in lifestyle,
formation of communities
where people influence each other,
utilization of media
to change the environmental culture of society.

And this is also the wisdom to cope with the living system.

The "wisdom for living system" that resides in "ancient civilizations" of humankind will revive.

Then, where is this kind of wisdom?

The wisdom to cope with
organizations, markets, and societies
evolving towards a "living system."
The wisdom to cope with the global environment
as a "gigantic living system."

From where should we learn about
the "wisdom to cope with the living system" and
the "wisdom for living system?"

The answer lies in a mysterious paradox.

The wisdom that resides in "ancient civilizations."

We should learn from it.

Because, in every country in the world,
ancient civilizations always embraced
the living system worldview in their foundations.

For example, as mentioned earlier,
it is told in the ancient Buddhist thought in Japan that
"in mountains, rivers, grass, trees, lands: everywhere
resides the Buddha nature, no matter where."

And the word "*Jinen*" in Japanese Buddhist thought.

It also expresses a deep philosophy related to
self organization and emergence.

Another example is the thought described by
the Native Americans,
"the earth, we are borrowing it from our descendents."
This is also the thought for living system
that transcends time and space.

Similarly, the religions and myths, legends and tales,
fables and fairy tales existing everywhere on earth.
They always describe the world we live in
as "the world as living system"
and tell us the wisdom for living in that world
through the heroes and heroines of those myths and tales.

In this way, in ancient civilizations of every country,
the wisdom for living systems richly abounds.

However, we often consider
"ancient civilizations" as "backward civilizations."
But that perception is incorrect.

Once the cultural anthropologist, Lévi-Strauss,
showed the keen insight into the pitfalls of
using the words "civilized" and "primitive."
He related that he found numerous examples of
outstanding wisdom
among those people whom we call "primitive."
Just as his thought expressed,
in the ancient civilizations sleep a lot of
superior wisdom for living systems.

Then, if so,
what will happen from now on?

The wisdom of "ancient civilization" will merge with the science and technology of "modern civilization" and will create a "new civilization."

The spiral development of civilization.

That will happen.

From now, the thought and wisdom for living system
which had resided in "ancient civilization"
will revive in a new form.
And this will merge with
science and technology,
organizations and institutions
which have been fostered in "modern civilization."

And this will be extremely important when
thinking about social changes and innovations
which humankind will need to deal with
in the 21st century.

Because science and technology, and
organizations and institutions
will be limited due to the thought and wisdom that
exist in their backgrounds.

For example, in the present age,
when we are faced with various problems,
we tend to lay the blame on
"science and technology," as well as "capitalism."
But, "science and technology" and "capitalism" themselves
are not the roots of these problems.

"Operationalism" in which we want to handle the world
according to the desire of our ego.
And the "mechanical system worldview"
in which we want the world to behave
like a machine that can be freely manipulated,
which is a projection of "operationalism."
Both of these factors existing in the background of
"science and technology" and "capitalism"
are precisely the roots of the problems.

That is, if the "science and technology" and "capitalism"
are combined with the "deep thought and wisdom,"
it would become a force greater than before
to generate coherence and empathy among many people,
to change their consciousness,
to change the culture of society,
and to change the society from its very foundation,
by spreading widely throughout all of society.

In particular, when the modern science and technology
combine with the ancient wisdom for living system,
a "new civilization" will be created right there.

For example, the Japanese thought of "*Mottainai*,"
which has globally spread through the advocacy of
the Nobel Peace Prize winner Wangari Maathai.
It considers resources as precious and to reuse them
without throwing them away, by using ancient wisdom.
When this good ancient thought is connected with
modern leading edge recycling technology,
the new "resource recycling civilization" of
the 21st century will be born.

Also, the "natural energy civilization" and the mature
"symbiotic civilization" of the new age will emerge.

**When the ancient "wisdom for living system" and
the modern "science and technology" merge together,
a great force for social change will be created.**

And the new civilization will not be one in which
the thought and wisdom for living system have been applied
only in the field of the "environment."

It will be a civilization in which
the thought and wisdom for living system have been applied
in various fields, such as "education," "communication,"
"community" and "medical care."

For example, the mind sensitive to the mysteries
residing in nature and to the wonders of nature, that is,
the thought of putting a high value on the mind,
namely the "sense of wonder"
as advocated by Rachel Carson.
When this thought is connected with educational systems
using leading edge technology including
high definition TV, 3D image and virtual reality,
a new paradigm of
"virtual experience-based nature education" will be born.

Also, the thought of putting a high value on that
people mutually communicate
the "tacit knowing" inexpressible in words
through images, without using languages.
When this thought of non-verbal communication
is connected with a sharing system of photos,
CGs, images and movies in the world of the Web,
a new paradigm of "image communication"
will be created.

Furthermore, the Japanese thought of
"Enishi" (a destined relationship),
which interprets meetings in life between people as
encounters that were "destined to happen" by something
and encounters that had some deep meaning.
When this thought is connected with
the culture of the Web community,
a new paradigm of "encounter community"
will be born.

And, the thought of *"Mitori"* (terminal care),
in which the dignity of persons passing away is respected
and family members watch over their last moments.
When this thought is connected with
the leading edge medical care systems,
a paradigm of "mind care hospice" with deep humanity
will be created.

In this way,
when the "deep thought and wisdom for living system"
residing in "ancient civilization" and
the "leading edge science, technology,
organizations and institutions"
fostered by "modern civilization"
connect and merge together,
we will see the birth of a "new social system" and
the birth of a "new paradigm civilization" right there.

However, if in each country, a spiral development between
ancient civilization and modern civilization occurs
in this way,
in fact, it can be foreseen that a spiral development
will occur on an even more magnificent scale.

What kind of spiral development will this be?

Spiral development will occur between "Eastern civilization" and "Western civilization."

The spiral development of
Eastern civilizations and Western civilizations.

This will happen.

Why?

Because, if in a country, a spiral development occurs
between ancient civilization and modern civilization,
then, the same kind of spiral development
will occur in humankind as a whole.

If so, what is the ancient civilization
in humankind as a whole?

"Eastern civilizations."

If we look back on the history of humankind,
the dawn of civilization began with
four Eastern civilizations:
Egyptian, Mesopotamian, Indus and the Yellow River.
And these civilizations were extremely
primitive civilizations from the viewpoint of
modern highly developed civilizations.
But in their foundations lay deep "religious grounds" and
the fertile thoughts for living system.

However, the center of the civilizations of humankind
shifted from there to the west.
The Western civilization first flowered in
Greece and Rome, then, with its center in Europe,
developed superior science and technology,
fostered sophisticated art and culture,
and created capitalism.

And, entering the 20th century, the center of that
civilization moved further to the west.
Because in a country called "America,"
which was founded in the New World
by immigrants from Europe,
science and technology flowered furthermore,
and capitalism achieved a rapid development.

That is, the "modern civilization" in humankind
as a whole is now "Western civilization"
centered in the West.

Consequently, what will happen from now
on a historical scale is the spiral development
and the interpenetration of
Eastern civilization and Western civilization.

The thought and wisdom for living system residing in
Eastern civilization will revive and will merge with
the leading edge "science and technology" and "capitalism"
fostered by Western civilization.

The spiral development will occur.

Then, in what way
will the merging of these two civilizations occur?

The merging of Eastern civilization with "science and technology" and "capitalism" has already begun.

Actually, this has already begun.

For example, Silicon Valley in the US.
This advanced region,
which should be called the leading edge of
"science and technology" and "capitalism" in the world.

When we enter a bookstore in this region,
we will notice something odd.

The shelves are laden with
books on science and technology
such as computer science and biotechnology,
books on business administration
such as venture business and management.

But oddly enough, beside them,
there are books which are always piled up.

Zen Buddhism, Taoism, esoteric Buddhism, and
Indian philosophy.

Such books on "Eastern thought" are always there.

What does it mean?

Also, in Europe,
the merging of both civilizations has begun.

For example, the Gaia thought mentioned earlier.
This new paradigm, the view of the Earth,
which has influenced environmental protection movements
around the world,
actually is a very Eastern view of the Earth as well.

And in the midst of the deepening of
the global environmental problems,
the German economist, Ernst Schumacher,
has become appreciated once again.
The thought of "small is beautiful" advocated by him
is also an Eastern thought.
"Buddhist economics" advocated by him symbolizes this.

Then, what is happening in Japan?

In this country as well, for a long time,
the merging of Western capitalism and Eastern thought
has been attempted.

This is so-called "Japanese style capitalism"
which is based on Eastern views of
work, compensation, organization, and talent.

For example, "working" in Japanese means
"for neighbors' happiness."
So, "Japanese style capitalism" is based on
such views of work.

And then, these trends to connect Eastern thought with
"science and technology" and "capitalism," in fact,
have begun to occur in various forms all over the world.

The age of
"prehistory" of humankind
will come to an end.

Then, in the history of humankind,
when Eastern civilization and Western civilization thus
achieve spiral development
and merge together,
what will happen in the future?

I dare to say,

The age of "prehistory" will come to an end.

That is, for the history of humankind,
the age of its "prologue" will end.

Because when Eastern civilization and
Western civilization merge together,
the most harmonized civilization
for humankind will be born.

"Science and technology" and "capitalism"
that have been developed by Western wisdom.
Thought and wisdom for living system
that have been deeply rooted in Eastern grounds.

When these two merge together,
a "new civilization" will come into the world.

And when opening the door to that "new civilization,"
we will obtain an important key
to solving such various problems for all humankind
as from the global environmental problems
to population explosion, food crisis, resource exhaustion,
energy crisis, as well as starvation, poverty,
discrimination, conflict, terrorism and war.

And some day,
when we have solved these problems
through the new civilization,
the prehistory for humankind will end.

From then,
the true history for humankind will begin.

The science fiction master, Arthur C. Clarke,
who passed away in 2008,
wrote a novel, *Childhood's End.*

As in that title,
we humankind will end our "childhood," some day.

It will be the moment
when we humankind make another great step towards
a new higher level on the spiral staircase of history.

12 Paradigm Shifts That Will Happen

The "voluntary economy" will increase its influence
on society relative to the "monetary economy."
And a new economic principle will emerge.

Many consumers and citizens
will come to participate in the process of
changes and innovations in society.

Direct democracy will be realized
not only in the field of "politics,"
but also in the fields of "economy" and "culture."

The mainstream of communication will shift
from linguistic communication
to image communication.

The culture that emphasizes "thinking"
and the culture that values "feeling"
will merge.

The "da Vinci society" will arrive,
where anyone can develop various talents
sleeping inside oneself.

The "post persona society" will arrive,
where anyone can express "multiple personalities"
hidden behind one's "persona."

The value system in society will shift
from "ideology" which emphasizes a single value
to "cosmology" which accepts diverse values.

The age of "exclusive monotheism" will end,
and the age of "new polytheism" will begin,
where various religions will coexist.

The basis of science will shift
from the "mechanical system worldview"
to the "living system worldview."

The merging will occur between
the "science and technology" of modern civilization and
the "wisdom for living system" of ancient civilization.

Eastern civilization and Western civilization
will learn from each other, and
a "new civilization" in the 21st century will be born.

Acknowledgements

This book was born from the recent activities of my lectures in Europe and the United States.

In 2007, at an invited lecture at the New School University in New York, I spoke about "How we can foresee the future" and "What we can foresee in the future," based on two books of mine published in Japan: *Dialectic Thinking* and *What Will Happen in the Future?*

In response to this lecture, many people in the audience said they would like me to publish in English the contents of the lecture. And then in 2008, after giving the keynote lecture at a conference of European innovators called iFest, many people once again said they would like to read the contents in English.

So I made up my mind to publish this book in English and Japanese simultaneously, adding the newly written chapter "The Future Foreseen by Dialectic Thinking—12 Paradigm Shifts That Will Happen in the Future of Human Society" to the contents of the two books mentioned above.

It is my hope that many people in the world will make use of the methods proposed in this book as "methods of wisdom" originated from Japan.

If you wish to listen to these two lectures, you could view videos of them at the website below:

www.sophiabank.co.jp/audio/english/tasaka/index.html

Finally, I would like to express my sincere appreciation to Mr. Jorge Pinto for editing and publishing the English version of this book. Without the destined encounter (*Deep Enishi*) with Mr. Pinto, this book could not come into the world. And I would also like to express my deep gratitude to Mr. Hisao Nishimiya, a translator, Mr. Tomoki Hotta of Babel Corporation and Professor Peter Skaer of Hiroshima University for dedicated cooperation in the translation of this book.

And I would like to express my appreciation to Ms. Kumi Fujisawa, co-founder of Think Tank SophiaBank. My dialogue with her inspired me and promoted the emergence of wisdom.

I also give deep thanks to my family, Sumiko, Sayer and Yue, for their watching warmly over me writing this book.

Lastly, I would like to dedicate this book to my father and mother who are not with us anymore. In a life filled with contradictions, they lived seeking deep meaning in those contradictions. The way they lived taught me the importance of living now to the full.

Hiroshi Tasaka
February 10, 2009

Publisher's Note

Translation of Japanese inspiration and insight into English can be a paradoxically impossible task: the more one strives to rigorously apply the rules of usage—such as how to apply definite and indefinite articles to nouns that may not bear them in the original—the more one clouds the prose or poetry with a Western sense of codification. Worrying over the difference or similarity between terms like "predict" and "foresee," or "discontinuity" and "non-linearity," can push the discussion so far into the left hemisphere of the brain that the purer concepts of the original are obscured. The reader is invited to open his or her mind to the underlying concept that is being argued; it is not unclear; allow this dialectic to involve not only the free exchange of ideas between thinkers, but between cultures as well.

Profile of the Author

Hiroshi Tasaka graduated from the Faculty of Engineering at the University of Tokyo with a Ph.D. in nuclear engineering in 1981.

From 1987, he worked as a visiting researcher at Battelle Memorial Institute and also at Pacific Northwest National Laboratories in the USA.

In 1990, he participated in founding the Japan Research Institute and engaged in "Industry Incubation" as a Chief Strategy Officer.

In 2000, he became a Professor at the Graduate School of Tama University in Tokyo and teaches students the philosophy, vision, policy, strategy, skills, mind and spirit of social entrepreneurs.

Also in 2000, he founded Think Tank SophiaBank, a "Paradigm Think Tank" whose mission is to change the "paradigms of social systems" in human society to solve the "global problems" and "frontier problems" for the society. In order to achieve this mission, SophiaBank formed a worldwide network that connects social entrepreneurs and acts as a "Socio-Incubator" that encourages social entrepreneurs to change old paradigms and to create new social systems.

In 2003, he established the Japan Social Entrepreneur Forum (JSEF) under SophiaBank to foster and support social entrepreneurs in order to bring about innovation and change in global society.

In 2006, he was nominated as a member of "US-Japan Innovators" by the Japan Society in New York.
Also, he was invited as a member of the Global Agenda Council of the World Economic Forum (Davos Meeting) in 2008.

Tasaka is a philosopher as well who has put forward a wide range of ideas and theories: the philosophy of life and work, of management and business; corporate and industrial strategies, social and government policies, a vision of the Internet revolution and the knowledge society, and also the paradigm shift in knowledge in human society.

He is the author of more than 50 books, including
The Age of Paradigm Shift;
Dialectic Thinking to Foresee the Future;
Wisdom of Complexity;
The Gaia Perspective; Ecology of Mind;
What Will Happen in the Knowledge Society?;
A New Paradigm of Strategic Thinking;
Management of Complex Systems;
Management of Tacit Knowing;
The Evolution of The Professional;
The Philosophy of Work; Why Do We Work?;
What is the Reward of Working?;
What is Success in Life?; and *To the Summit -*
Why Should You Embrace an Ideal in Your Heart?.

tasaka@hiroshitasaka.jp
http://www.hiroshitasaka.jp/
http://www.sophiabank.co.jp/

Printed in the United Kingdom by
Lightning Source UK Ltd., Milton Keynes
141623UK00001B/113/P